Jeanne

Keep moving throughout
your life.

Jane Gardner Birch

THEY FLEW PROUD

Jane Gardner Birch

Published by Jane Gardner Birch

Printed in the United States of America by Evangel Press, P.O. Box 189, Nappanee, Indiana 46550-0189. Call 800-253-9315 for single or bulk (discounted) purchase.

Edited and page layout by Amy Clingensmith.
Cover design by Matt Gable of Evangel Press.

Library of Congress Control Number: 2007934900

ISBN 10: 1-933858-25-7
ISBN 13: 978-1-933858-25-8

CONTENTS

DEDICATION

*"The Wright Brothers
created the single greatest cultural force
since the invention of writing.
The airplane became the first World Wide Web,
bringing people, languages, ideas and values together."*
• Bill Gates, Microsoft co-founder and philanthropist

The Civilian Pilot Training Program
(pre- to post-WWII) trained tens of thousands
of new pilots all across the U.S.
The airplane brought my father, Gardner Birch, to the CPTP,
the Grove City Airport and to the students on the Boards.
The common passion for flying connected them all.
Lessons learned while flying expanded their horizons,
their ideas and their values,
and taught them they could soar anywhere.
With my research of the CPTP and the students on the Boards,
with the input of dozens of people from all over,
and with the help of technology and the World Wide Web,
They flew Proud was created.
The story is universal, for anyone,
and no knowledge of aviation is needed to learn and enjoy.

This is for you Dad,
and your students on the Boards.

FOREWORD

The Civilian Pilot Training Program (also known as the CPTP, and later War Training Service, or WTS) was the legislative culmination of what has come to be known as the Golden Age of Aviation. The Golden Age has been characterized as consisting of famous aviators, record flights, air racing and exhibition flying. Newspaper headlines heralded the new and exciting technology that grew to epic proportions from The Great War (1914-1918) to the end of the 1930s. Another way of looking at the Golden Age would be to interpret it as a period of growth for aviation's infrastructure, with considerable governmental assistance. This period saw the inception of the air mail service, first flown by military pilots in 1918 and continued by the U.S. Post Office until 1925, when it was taken over by civilian contractors. Other notable legislative achievements were the passages of the Air Commerce Act of 1926, which inaugurated federal regulation of aviation, and the Civil Aeronautics Act of 1938, which transferred jurisdiction for civil aviation from the Department of Commerce to a fully independent agency.

The Civilian Pilot Training Program, which was designed to create a pool of civilian pilots in the event of war and stimulate the private flying industry, fits into the concept of interpreting the Golden Age as an era of federal stimulation of aviation through financial support and regulatory legislation. Originated in 1939, the CPTP was one of the largest federally funded vocational education programs in history. In its original formulation, the program had two goals: (1) to provide initial training for pilots and thereby build up the pool of available aviators in the event of war; and (2) to stimulate the light-plane industry and private flying, which were perceived to have languished as more and more priority had been given to commercial and military aviation. The goals of the CPTP soon changed as a result of World War II, and the program did not fulfill the intentions of Robert H. Hinckley, chair of the Civil Aeronautics Authority, the program's originator. Nevertheless, it contributed significant numbers of pilots to the war effort and broke new ground in training women and African Americans.

While the CPTP has been written about in terms of its legislative and political history, readers have hitherto not been exposed to the countless personal stories that arose as a result of its impact throughout the country. Over the years, I have been regaled with such recollections and it has made me realize that the CPTP indeed had another, more intimate connection to the lives of American citizens. Now we have Jane Birch's *They Flew Proud*, a crisply told account of her father, Gardner Birch, his fellow pilots and their involvement in the CPTP-WTS course of training at Grove City College, in Grove City, a small town in Western Pennsylvania. Ms. Birch has done a remarkable job of piecing the story together so many years after the fact. She deserves a great deal of credit for what obviously has been a labor of love, a resounding tribute to her father and his love of aviation, and a reawakening of formative childhood memories.

● *Dominick A. Pisano*
Author of "To Fill the Skies with Pilots:
The Civilian Pilot Training Program, 1939-1946"
Smithsonian Institution Press, Washington, D.C., 2001

It started with a question many years ago: "What ever happened to the Grove City Airport?" As I would drive home to Hermitage in Western Pennsylvania, I'd take the PA Turnpike to Interstate 79 North toward Erie. There are two exits off I-79 to Grove City. Once, I exited during daylight, stopped at a gas station, asked if there was still an airport and where it was. I was directed to the current airport, but nothing looked familiar. A large chain link, gated fence blocked a lengthy entrance; it was locked for the evening. That was several years ago. I left knowing that this was not the airport of my childhood when, 55 years ago, weekend visits to the airport, the hangar, the men, the planes, the wind sock and taxi rides, created some of my most cherished memories that a young child of those times could have. It was my personal Disneyland.

Then in March of 2004 came a second question from friends who were visiting my house. They came into my bedroom and saw a picture I

have of my dad, Gardner Birch, in a military uniform and hat with a winged badge from the World War II era. Bob asked, "When was your dad in the service?" And by rote I answered, "He was never in the service, he trained pilots to fly at the Grove City Airport." I look back at the ignorance and ridiculousness of my answer! But as I looked daily at that picture, Bob's question kept coming back.

I couldn't discount or ignore that uniform! My father had died 42 years ago, having given up his beloved flying career 14 years before his death. And now it was clear; I knew nothing about that part of his life. In April of that year, I searched the Internet for answers to many questions, issues and relationships that had sidetracked me for years. I found initial information about the Civilian Pilot Training Program and even e-mailed an elderly former flight instructor, Chuck Franklyn, who had a web page about his CPTP involvement. And that summer, I discovered there was a Grove City Airport, listed with a phone number. But, as usual, life's events again pulled me away.

I was going home in October of 2004. The weekend before, I called the airport. Noel Dean, a mechanic, returned my call and informed me that the old airport, with its grass runway, no longer existed. The current one replaced it around 1974. Then he said, "But the Boards are here. They were saved when the old airport was torn down and list 127 student pilots' names and solo dates, from the summer of 1944 to the summer of 1948: 15 females and 112 males. And there is an 80-year-old who comes here and flies, and he says he was an instructor there." I asked, "What is his name?" Noel answered, "Rocky Filer." I knew that name … from deep inside it surfaced from 55 years ago.

Finding Rocky, having him show me the Boards (that were my father's creation), the old airport site and hearing about the men and women whose names were as familiar to me as favorite characters in children's books brought back a past I thought would never be available to me again. Few get the chance to relive part of their childhood through adult eyes. I was launching an intimate search for new knowledge of my father and his flying life related to the airport, WWII, the men and women on the Boards and our roots in Western Pennsylvania. Was there a story here beyond nostalgia? Had any of this made a lasting imprint or impact? Now in my 60s, I see life is complex, not black and white; everyone has strengths, flaws and potential secrets. Could I handle it emotionally, especially if the reality I discovered was at odds with what I remembered? Would the idealized, possibly naive, character picture I had of my dad stand up under intense scrutiny? This was a risk I had to take.

Over the next few months, an adventure unfolded spontaneously, like nothing I've ever experienced. I located, interviewed and became friends with about 35 of the 127 Board pilots (and met 15 at a reunion), then another 40 or more of the other's most immediate kin and many related parties. From these interviews, the Board stories in Part II of this book were created (a student is not written about if there is no information about him or her). Pictures, stories, memorabilia and leads began pouring into me. Local historic societies (Grove City, Greenville, Mercer County and Crawford County) had pertinent information. Humbly, I became the organizer only. This story, the pictures and everything about it belongs to the people and events referenced in the following pages. I thank them for their trust in me "to do them proud in the telling."

● *Jane Gardner Birch*

PART I:

THE CIVILIAN PILOT TRAINING PROGRAM

CHAPTER 1

Humble Beginnings - Lofty Dreams

Not everything of importance in World War II happened overseas. Yes, that's where the drama, bravado, horror and battles occurred. But overseas was only half of the history. Like a good marriage, forces abroad needed a partner in sync both in regards to vision and goals. The action was "over there," but the support and production were "over here." The United States triumphed in the Atlantic and Pacific arenas because of efforts the soldiers received from those back home. Not everyone could be active military, but all could be active. Unsung, and usually without fanfare, the average American, left at home, was vital to the cause.

Rationing, shortages, war bonds and FDR were all a part of everyday life in the spring of 1943, a turning point in my dad's life. It had taken five years using his quiet mind to construct this plan, paid for by laying brick after brick after brick. He was too old to join the regular military. But once the family bills were met and his first house was purchased with a five-year note, any spare money paid for a few more flying hours in his logbook (276 total hours/200 required.) Now at 33, Gardner Birch #66923 could list his occupation on the Civil Aeronautics Authority (CAA) form as an apprentice flight instructor. He took his flight test at Grove City Airport in a Piper J-3 with a Lycoming 65 engine. Report remarks were, "Flight technique very good, oral instruction above average." He could now teach the cadets of the Civilian Pilot Training Program (CPTP) the basics of flying for their country's freedom.

Gardner Birch was born in Sharon, Pa., part of scenic Mercer County, in 1910. That part of northwestern Pennsylvania, abutting the Shenango River, is halfway between Pittsburgh and Erie and borders the Ohio Line. In the 1800s, Sharon attracted heavily from all of Europe, especially the many small ethnic countries, and the British Isles. Immigrants, with strong work ethics, arrived willing to do any physical labor in agriculture, saw and grist mills, iron and coal mines, steel mills, blast furnaces, on railroads, utilities, and many supporting heavy and light industries. The area also offered abundant wildlife for fishing and hunting. Sharon's economy has always been fragile. Per the 2000 census, its median household income was $26,945, Mercer County's was $34,666, and the nation's was $41,994. On December 28, 2005, "The Herald" newspaper in Sharon claimed, "The future of domestic steel-industry jobs, including those in the Shenango Valley, hinges on whether President Bush backs up federal trade regulators and imposes a quota to stem a sudden surge of Chinese steel pipe imports." Bush did not impose the quota. "Bling" is only a word heard on television in Sharon; it's not part of everyday life there. People tend to live within their means. Economic uncertainty breeds a frugality. Yet the county had a stable environment for growing up, with tried-and-true blue-collar values: work ethic, family, loyalty, frugality, honesty, integrity and helping others.

Robert and Mae Gardner Birch were just kids themselves when they married and had their first child, a daughter LaRada, in 1907. Three years later, Gardner was born, followed by Robert in 1914. Robert was a bricklayer by trade, but after the birth of three children, divorce drove a deep fracture permanently into the young family. The two boys remained with their dad, and LaRada went with her mother to nearby New Castle. The estrangement would be lifelong. By 1925 Robert had remarried, and he and Edith were expecting a baby, Barbara Jean. To help with family expenses, Gardner joined his dad in bricklaying in his mid-teens. He continued to live at home, paying rent each month and even paying for college for his brother, Bob.

Nothing extraordinary about this, it was the Depression, and you did everything you could to help your family. And when you could, you sneaked in a little fun. Dad had a good sense of humor, a natural curiosity and was social. He did things with the guys, and went on double and triple dates, as well as fished, hunted, swam at the river, picnicked, listened to sports on the radio, took in an occasional movie, played cards and

Gardner and Grace Birch pose together in the late 1930s.

went for rides in a car. In the late 1930s he met my mother, Grace Jones. She was the youngest of four children of Frank and Margaret Titus Jones. The Jones lineage was from Wales; the Titus (de Vries) line was Dutch. Margaret's father had a large farm several miles east of town on what was called Dutch Lane.

When Grace became pregnant, Gardner married her on June 29, 1938. On January 31, 1939, Grace went into labor. The full-term baby boy was breach. Delivery was difficult. Dr. Dan Phythyon, put Mom "under," then used force and forceps – practices that were standard for the times. The unnamed baby lived less than an hour. Both the doctor and my father signed the death certificate, which cited "trauma (to the head) incident to breach extraction," as the cause of death. With usual efficiency, Dad handled all details of the tragedy. Baby Birch was buried in Oakwood Cemetery, in less than 24 hours, with my mother still in the hospital. Mom, who had difficulty showing emotions, did not talk about this. She only told us that the baby was stillborn; she may have never been told the truth herself. "It would be easier on her." She carried the unspoken pain inside her the rest of her life.

At the same time Gardner was coming of age, aviation had taken wings. Not a single human being had ever flown a powered aircraft when the 20th century began. The first piloted, powered, controlled flight (by the Wright Brothers in 1903) lasted 12 seconds and carried one man (Orville) 120 feet. Within three days of Gardner's birth in 1910, Glenn H. Curtiss flew a Hudson Flyer 135.4 miles, from Albany to New York City, in two hours and 32 minutes. In 1918, U.S. Army pilots in Curtiss JN4-H Jennies, begin continuous scheduled public-service airmail between N.Y.C. and D.C., via Philly. In the very first airmail flight, the pilot misread his compass and flew 180 degrees in the wrong direction and landed in Virginia instead of New York City. The mail made the rest of the trip by train. Planes were drafted for military service in World War I by the Allies and Central Powers to do individual combat with their enemies. Manfred von Richthofen, often using a Fokker Dr. I triplane painted bright red with black crosses edged in white, became Germany's Red Baron hero. He was the most successful fighter pilot of WWI, credited with 80 confirmed air combat victories. He was ultimately brought down, and men of courage like Eddie Rickenbacker and Billy Mitchell become the United States' new military warriors.

America survived the "war to end all wars." The Roaring '20s brought a booming national economy and flights that were headline events. Manufacturers increased plane speed and capabilities and pilots reacted with new quickness, endurance and maneuverability records. During this time, Mercer County's most famous aviator become known nationally. As a young boy, Oakley G. Kelly moved with his parents to Grove City, where his father operated a feed store. Young Kelly went to local school and three years at Grove City College before enlisting in the Army Air Corps, becoming a flying cadet, then a test pilot at McCook Air Force Base. His most famous exploit occurred in May of 1923: Kelly and Lt. John

An Oakley G. Kelly montage hangs at the Grove City Airport.

McCready flew a Fokker T-2 Transport form New York to San Diego, the first nonstop, transcontinental flight of 2,600-plus miles in 26 hours and 50 minutes. Later he would land at local fields (including Grove City) when visiting his parents.

Fred "Posy" Thompson, in his mid-80s and living in Erie, Pa., was from that area. He recalls, "My father parked me on the wing of Kelly's plane. I was 5 years old at the time (1926) and it made a strong impression on me that I can clearly remember 80 years later. That is when I caught 'The Disease' (the desire and love to fly). The field is about three miles west of Forestville and I think about it every time I pass by. There is more than meets the eye in Kelly's record. This aircraft was a state-of-the-art transport plane owned by the U.S. Army. It was powered by a 400-horsepower/12-cylinder Liberty engine. The pilot sat outside beside the engine. There was a second set of controls inside the cabin and the pilots could change places using a door in the left front of the cabin. The flight was made from east to west into the prevailing westerly winds, which looks like a stupid thing to do. Not so because of the huge fuel load needed to make this long flight. The heavily loaded T-2 could not climb over the mountains east of San Diego. However, when headed west from New York, the eastern mountains could be surmounted with full tanks. Even then, it was touch and go, as the liquid-cooled Liberty engine overheated with only a few miles to go. All available liquid (including urine) was poured into the radiator of the engine and they just squeaked into Rockwell Field. They covered 2,650 miles and used 593 gallons of gasoline."

In 1927, a tickertape parade with four million people celebrated 25-year-old Charles Lindbergh's first nonstop solo transatlantic flight from N.Y.C. to Paris (3,600 miles in 33.5 hours) in his Ryan monoplane, The Spirit of St. Louis. He embodied conquering new frontiers through flight. According to daughter Reeve Lindbergh in 1999, "Overnight celebrity followed him home from Paris to the U.S. and around the nation on his tour promoting aviation. Fame followed him on his goodwill tour to Mexico late in 1927, where he met the U.S. ambassador's daughter Anne Morrow, who he married in 1929. They traveled all over the world as pioneer aviator-explorers, mapping air routes for the fledgling airline industry. Together they navigated by the stars and watched the great surfaces of the earth revealed beneath their wings. People still tell me exactly where they were standing when they heard the news of his landing in Paris. Generations of pilots still talk of his influence upon their careers."

The Great Depression hit the nation's economy like a bomb in October of 1929. When the stock market crashed, the small mill towns in Mercer County were spared until the aftershocks. Steel orders began to dwindle until plants, the life blood of the communities, were forced to shut down. Some local banks closed their doors. Many lost their jobs, farms, homes, savings and hope. There was no unemployment compensation or welfare. Families pooled meager wages to survive. The poor were poorer and many wealthy investors joined the ranks of debtors. Panic, helplessness and hard times cast a shroud, even in the Shenango Valley. The government had to step up under FDR and legislate a New Deal to lift the nation's spirit through fireside chats, growth and experimental programs. It was a long, grueling climb toward recovery and normalcy. Interest and advancements in aviation were adrenaline rushes for citizens hungry for good news. Amelia Earhart made the first female-led transatlantic flight in 1932 from Newfoundland to Ireland in 15 hours and 18 minutes. Then in '35 she made the first solo flight by a woman from Hawaii to California. Magnate Howard Hughes sets a transcontinental speed record in '37, followed in '38 by an around-the-world flight in a Lockheed "14" in three days and 19 hours. There were many experienced WWI fighter pilots who were eager to show off their new skills. Many became barnstormers (Lindbergh started this way), flying into small towns, showing off their flying skills and taking paying passengers for rides. They got organized, and a series of air shows sprang up around the country, with air races, aerobatics and feats of air superiority. Flying was now local for anyone wanting challenge and adventure, and not afraid of the risk.

Right after his marriage in mid-1938, and prepped for that challenge, my dad began flying lessons in a Piper Cub at the Sharon Air Service in Brookfield, Ohio, given by seasoned instructor Judd Youkers.

From there he took more hours at Bernard Airport in Youngstown from Michael Kardos. The country was in recession; industrial production was down 33 percent and national income was down 12 percent. Flying then, as now, was expensive. There were no credit cards. It was pay as you go, with lessons of 20 or 30 minutes, and lessons meant giving up something else to get them. Gardner Birch was practical, not frivolous, and he had a plan. War seemed closer, and there was talk

that the U.S didn't have enough planes or pilots. After those first seven hours, he added 100 hours by July of '41. Japan's attack on Pearl Harbor in December launched the U.S. into the most costly war ever in terms of human life. In another 10 months (May of 1942), Gardner had 165 total hours while taking ground-school courses at Youngstown and Westminster colleges. And family life weighed heavier now. He had been a bricklayer for 17 years, and yet was just 32 years old. He and Grace were the parents of two young girls, with one more on the way, and had just bought their first house. Grace's father was dying of cancer and she was helping to nurse him. But Dad was focused on his goal.

On a parallel path was 30-year-old Murl DeArment, also a young father living in Sharon, working at Sharon Tube, and taking flying lessons from Judd in Ohio. The DeArments were a pioneering blacksmith family in Crawford County, just to the north. They made high-quality farrier tools that developed into Channellock. Murl's father was a caretaker and game keeper at the Huidekoper horse farm on Conneaut Lake in 1912, when Murl was born there. The Huidekopers descended from Harm Jan Huidekoper of the Holland Company, which had lent money to the government during the Revolution and had been paid back in large tracts of land in western New York and northwestern Pennsylvania. In 1815, Harm Jan moved to Meadville and took charge of the company's affairs, gaining prominence and respect. He bought up much of the unsold acreage, creating a large personal fortune, which he passed down to his heirs. Third-generation "A.C." (Arthur Clarke) Huidekoper established The Little

Missouri Stock Company, probably the largest horse stables in the U.S. around the turn of the 20th century. The horses were bred on North Dakota ranches and brought to Conneaut Lake for breaking, training and sale. For a Christmas present in 1914, A.C. gave toddler Murl (nicknamed "Fuzzy") the book "Little Rhymes for Little Readers" by Wilhelmina Seegmiller, and signed it "To my little Chestnutting friend, Merry Xmas from A.C. Huidekoper."

Fuzzy's family moved to Sharon so his father could find work in a steel mill in Masury, Ohio. At 15 in 1927, Fuzzy quit high school (like Dad) and began work at Sharon Tube, living at home and modestly helping the family economy. Within a few years he met Martha George from neighboring Sharpsville. Martha's grandfather owned George Electric, which was next to the Ritz Theatre on Main Street at Second. She and her friends got to see movies for free if they went through a door in the back alley from the electric shop. Martha and Fuzzy hung out in a crowd and began double dating, going for barbeques and for rides in cars.

On September 10, 1932, after Martha graduated from high school, they got married. Their daughter, Ella May, was born on June 19, 1933, and was just a toddler when Fuzzy became interested in flying. He started lessons in a Piper Cub with Jack Harper in Five Points, Ohio, then flew with Judd Youkers in Brookfield. Fuzzy, the steel worker, added hour after hour until he, too, had his flight instructor's rating.

Just 20 miles south of Sharon is the town of New Castle and a property abandoned and overgrown by weeds. Findley "Fin" Wilson, with a

A.C. Huidekoper gave a copy of 'Little Rhymes for Little Readers' to Murl DeArment for Christmas in 1914.

vision in his mind, leased the land in 1932 and turned it into the New Castle Airport. Fin was born on the family homestead in Princeton Pa., in Slippery Rock Township in 1906. At age 12, he saw his first airplane while living on that farm. He graduated from New Castle High School in 1924 and went with the tradition of the one safe profession: teaching. He was unaware of his instinctive, strong business sense. Enrolling in Slippery Rock State Teachers College, Fin earned 12 teaching credits and taught eight grades in local schools for 11 years. But teaching school wasn't as intriguing as flying, and when the

Depression came along, it wasn't financially profitable.

So he went to work for the Franklin Aircraft Co. in Franklin, Pa. It was a private corporation that used a vacant space in the Joy Manufacturing Company complex (now Joy Global, makers of mining equipment and a member of the NASDAQ 100). Fin got his first introduction to aviation at the age of 23 in 1929 and told a local reporter in 1983: "Flying was expensive, but I figured if I went to work at the aircraft factory I could get 40 cents an hour." He bought his first airplane before he had ever ridden in one, the Franklin Sport Trainer. This first version was a two-place, open cockpit, tandem bi-plane powered by a 65-horse-power, five-cylinder Lambert radial engine with a top speed of 100 miles per hour. It was 20 feet long, had a wingspan of 26 feet and weighed 850 pounds; only 12 were manufactured and sold. Later, five 90-horsepower Sport 90s were built, with a 120-mph speed. The test pilot at the factory taught Fin how to fly and he first soloed in Franklin during the summer of 1930. Of the original 65s, three owners died in crashes. Fin was lucky or well-taught or both. Suffering the effects of the Depression, Franklin Aircraft went bankrupt in 1932. Few planes survived. One known model, No. 8, is in pieces waiting possible restoration, and the local Experimental Aircraft Association Chapter #988 has a copy of the original Sport plans.

In the fall of 1930, Fin flew to Florida to operate the Fort Lauderdale Airport for the winter. At that time, the airport was merely a grassy field.

"During World War II, it was swallowed up by what is now the international airport." Next he headed to California to work for Century Pacific Airlines. That was short-lived; jobs were scarce, and pilots were laid off. Fin returned home to teaching. "In 1932, the school board went broke, and I taught for four months without a dime." It was that year he leased the airport property – a smart way to leverage his hard-to-come-by teaching wages. He opened the New Castle Flying School and built a large 60-by-200-foot hangar. Next he had to promote and sell. He wowed and inspired youngsters by landing on the football field at Slippery Rock College. Bob McGowan remembers skipping school as a child to see Fin take off and land on that field. Bob dreamed of flying himself one day, and he did. Fin enthused others with lessons. Among his flying students was Maxine Anderson of New Castle, whom he married in 1937. She was the first woman to fly solo in the county and was the first student to use the New Castle Airport for her solo flight. Both Fin and Maxine soon had commercial licenses with flight instructor's ratings: the basic requirements of the CPTP instructor. The hangar was expanded to include an office, an apartment and an ice cream stand that Maxine ran. On his own time in the air, he flew the initial mail out of New Castle. For that, Fin was rewarded with a nice pair of gold wings with a small mail bag hanging in the center. He was also known to bombard school-yards with candy eggs from airplanes during Easter. Fin had built his first airport and flying school. He had tasted success and wanted more.

CAA chairman Robert Hinckley, right, 'talks shop' with Orville Wright in 1938. Hinckley led the founding of the Civilian Pilot Training Program in '39. / Photo courtesy of Hinckley Institute of Politics

CHAPTER 2

The Birth of the CPTP and the Airport

Starting in 1937, world tensions were palpable and could be keenly felt in the United States. The nation witnessed Japan's flagrant acts of aggression in China, then Germany taking over Austria. President Roosevelt was fully aware that many Americans were isolationists with their heads in the sand. Even though the U.S. had adopted an official policy of neutrality, FDR was observant and kept a wary eye on events unfolding in Europe and Asia for several years preceding WWII. "Let no one imagine that America will escape, that it may expect mercy, that this Western Hemisphere will not be attacked." In practical terms, FDR knew how difficult it would be for simultaneous wars in Europe and Asia, especially with America's sagging aerial capacities. The aggressors were far superior in numbers of military aircraft and in pilots to man them. Despite pockets of resistance, Roosevelt gave the green light to a new military expansion.

The Civil Aeronautics Act of 1938 contained language authorizing and funding a trial program for what would evolve into the Civilian Pilot Training Program (CPTP). FDR unveiled the program on December 27, 1938, announcing at a White House press conference that he had signed off on a proposal to provide a needed boost to general aviation by providing pilot training to 20,000 college students a year. The brainchild of Robert H. Hinckley, a quintessential New Deal administrator, the CPTP was the first full-scale, federally funded aviation education program and one of the largest government-sponsored vocational educational programs of its time. It would use the classrooms of American colleges and universities and the facilities of local flying schools certified by the CAA, be supported by government funds and provide a pool of young civilian pilots who could be available for military service if war came. If a young cadet with only basic flight training could land a plane in peril, lives and money could be saved. Dominick A. Pisano, curator of the National Air and Space Museum of the Smithsonian Institute, nailed the purpose of the CPTP with his book's title "To Fill the Skies with Pilots."

Hinckley also believed these youth would be more "air-minded" and trained for future employment in the aviation industry. A boost would be given to the depressed light-plane industry and to fixed base operators who provid-

```
                                                                    #157
                    CIVIL AERONAUTICS AUTHORITY
                         WASHINGTON, D. C.

Bulletins covering                                      June 4, 1940
non-college, instruc-
tor and refresher
courses available

                THE CIVILIAN PILOT TRAINING PROGRAM - 1940-41
                PRELIMINARY COURSE (PRIVATE) COLLEGIATE PHASE
                              (SUMMER SESSION)

                          GENERAL INFORMATION

     The Civilian Pilot Training Act of 1939 authorizes the Civil Aero-
nautics Authority to conduct a program for the training of civilian pilots
through educational institutions and pursuant to such regulations as the
Authority may prescribe.  The preliminary phase of the program calls for
sufficient training to prepare a student for a private pilot certificate.
The course is divided into two parts:  A 72-hour ground course given at
the participating institution, and a 35 to 50-hour flight course given at
a nearby airport by an operator or operators whom the institution may se-
lect, subject to approval by the Authority.  The preliminary course for
the summer of 1940 will start June 15 and must be completed by September
15.
```

Pilot training for civilians was born under the Civil Aeronautics Act of 1938.

ed services such as flying lessons, chartered flights and aircraft sales, as well as maintenance, fuel and supplies. And it would pave the way for a post-war boom in private flying by providing a ready-made source of pilots who would spur demand for recreational aircraft. These dimensions were distinctly New Deal in philosophy. By pumping money into the light aviation industry and small airport operations, the CPTP would realize the New Deal goal of providing economic aid to business enterprises affected by the Depression.

Legislators, the aviation industry and the military were skeptical. Although they had been consulted and given tentative approval, the Army and Navy, both directly affected, were tacitly suspicious that the civilian CAA would have administrative control over pre-training of military pilots. Yet they acknowledged they were ill-equipped to produce pilots in mass numbers. Isolationists and non-interventionists screamed it was a militarist plot to embroil the U.S. in war. Only the general public seemed to favor the plan.

One of Hinckley's goals of the CPTP was to aid the light-plane industry. The U.S. faced just as large a shortage of civilian training aircraft as it did civilian pilots. CAA (predecessor of the Federal Aviation Administration) regulations required a CPTP-participating flight school to own one aircraft for every 10 students enrolled in the program. Furthermore, the requirements specified for these aircraft narrowed the field to only several models in production at that time, with most flight schools preferring tandem-seat configurations of the Piper Cub (dual controls with a front seat for the instructor and a back seat for the student). Seizing the opportunity, several light aircraft manufacturers – WACO, Meyers, Aeronca and Taylorcraft – quickly filled the market void with CPTP-compatible aircraft.

The CPTP's demonstration program began in February of '39 at 13 colleges and universities that were selected either for their pioneer work in aeronautical engineering or because of flight training programs already in place. In October 1939, the full-scale program got under way. And not a moment too soon, for on September 1, 1939, German forces invaded Poland. Within days, France, the United Kingdom, Australia, New Zealand and Canada joined in declaring war on Hitler. World War II had begun. Could the Civilian Pilot Training Program produce the numbers the U.S. military so desperately needed?

On May 26, 1940, at 9:30 p.m. EST from the White House, President Franklin Delano Roosevelt addressed the nation by radio. "There are many among us who in the past closed their eyes to events abroad—because they believed in utter good faith what some of their fellow Americans told them—that what was taking place in Europe was none of our business, that no matter what happened over there, the United States could always pursue its peaceful and unique course in the world. There are many

Public—No. 153—76th Congress
Chapter 244—First Session

An Act
to provide for the training of civil aircraft pilots, and for other purposes

Be it enacted by the Senate and House of Representatives of the United States of America in Congress assembled, That this Act may be cited as the "Civilian Pilot Training Act of 1939."

SEC. 2. The Civil Aeronautics Authority is authorized, within the limits of available appropriations made by the Congress, to train civilian pilots or to conduct programs for such training, including studies and researches as to the most desirable qualifications for aircraft pilots. Such training or programs shall be conducted pursuant to such regulations as such Authority may from time to time prescribe, including regulations requiring students participating therein to maintain appropriate insurance and to pay such laboratory or other fees for ground-school training, not exceeding $40 per student, as the Authority may deem necessary or desirable;

Provided, That in the administration of this Act, none of the benefits of training or programs shall be denied on account of race, creed, or color. Such training or programs may be carried out either through the use of the facilities and personnel of the Authority or by contracts with educational institutions or other persons (as defined in section 1 (27) of the Civil Aeronautics Act of 1938).

SEC. 3. At least 5 per centum of the students selected for training under this Authority shall be selected from applicants other than college students.

SEC. 4. The Authority is authorized to lease or accept loans of such real property, and to purchase, lease, exchange, or accept loans of such personal property, as may be necessary or desirable for carrying out the provisions of this Act.

SEC. 5. For the purposes of carrying out its functions under this Act, the Authority is authorized to exercise all powers conferred upon it by the Civil Aeronautics Act of 1938 and to appoint and fix the compensation of experienced instructors, airmen, medical and other professional examiners and experts in training and research without regard to the provisions of other laws applicable to the employment and compensation of officers and employees of the United States. The provisions of section 3709 of the Revised Statutes shall not apply to contracts with educational institutions and other persons for the use of aircraft or other facilities or for the performance of services authorized by section 2 of this Act.

SEC. 6. Any executive department of independent establishment is hereby authorized to cooperate with the Authority in carrying out the purposes of this Act, and for such purposes may lend or transfer to the Authority, by contract or otherwise, or if so requested by the Authority, lend to educational institutions or other persons cooperating with the Authority in the conduct of any such training or program, civilian officials, or employees, aircraft and other property or equipment, and lands or buildings under its control and in excess of its own requirements.

SEC. 7. There is hereby authorized the sum of $5,675,000 for the purpose of carrying out the provisions of this Act during the fiscal years 1939 and 1940 and not to exceed the sum of $7,000,000 during each subsequent fiscal year. This Act shall expire on July 1, 1944, and all contracts, leases, or other obligations entered into under this Act shall expire on or prior to such date:

Provided, That no alien shall receive training under the provisions of this Act.

Approved, June 27, 1939.

The Civilian Pilot Training Act was put into practice in 1939.

President Roosevelt addresses the nation via radio in May 1940.

among us who closed their eyes, from lack of interest or lack of knowledge, honestly and sincerely thinking that the many hundreds of miles of salt water made the American hemisphere so remote that the people of North and Central and South America could go on living in the midst of their vast resources without reference to, or danger from, other continents of the world. ... To those who have closed their eyes for any of these many reasons, to those who would not admit the possibility of the approaching storm ... I do not

share those illusions. ... Yes, we have spent large sums of money on the national defenses. This money has been used to make our Army and Navy today the largest, the best equipped and the best trained peace-time military establishment in the whole history of this country." The CPTP was now an integral piece of the military puzzle.

On December 12, 1941, five days after the Japanese attack on Pearl Harbor, President Roosevelt, with the U.S. now fully engaged in WWII, signed Executive Order 8974, transforming the CPTP into a wartime program under the War Training Service (WTS). All WTS graduates were now required to sign a contract agreeing to enter the military following graduation. In the five years between 1939 and 1944, the Civilian Pilot Training Program trained 435,165 people, including women and African Americans. Beginning in 1939, one woman could be trained for every 10 men. But in June of '41, women were banned from participating. Notable pilots trained under the program were astronaut and Senator John Glenn, top Navy ace Alexander Vraciu, Douglas test pilot Robert Rahn, top American WWII ace Major Richard Bong, WASP Dora Dougherty and Tuskegee Airman Maj. Robert Deiz.

Back in New Castle, Fin Wilson was very aware of the big bucks being paid to the flight contractors, half of the CPTP training team. He started out doing all the flight instruction himself. Then after the U.S. declared war, he hired more instructors to help train cadets. The government paid him $325 per student for 10 hours of flying, while the colleges got less than $50 per student for 72 hours of instruction. The government furnished the airplanes, and one certified aircraft of not less than 50 horsepower was required for each 10 students. These aircraft had to be based at the airport of instruction; ferrying them back and forth to other training centers was not permitted. The New Castle Airport could house 30 planes, and for security reasons, they were required to be hangared each night. One flight instructor was required for each 15 students, and he had responsibility for them throughout the course. "The number of trainees assigned to any operator on one airport will be limited to 60." The flight contractor was required to carry $50/100,000 public liability and $5,000 property damage insurance on each student (a $12.75 premium). Students had to be between 18 and 26 years old and meet the physical requirements for a student's pilot's certificate of commercial CPT grade. The ground instruction contractor (or college) was responsible for providing transportation to the airport, which had to be within 10 miles or 30 minutes legal driving time (not to exceed 45 miles per hour) of the institution. "Under no consideration shall students be allowed to 'hitch hike,' a practice which shall be deemed grounds for discontinuing students from training." Fin's New Castle Airport was set to catch the wave of profiting from military preparedness – very acceptable to do because it was also patriotic. Why not replicate and catch another wave?

The town of Grove City sits 30 miles southeast of Sharon. It is similar in many ways, yet different. Its humble beginnings as the Village of Pine Grove began in 1798 when Mary and Valentine Cunningham settled on the banks of Wolf Creek

CPTP instructors wore a CAA/War Training pin on their formal dress hats.

and built a grist mill. Most villages in Mercer County were settled by a river or stream with a mill. Grist mills were usually built first so farmers could grind their grain. Sawmills followed to provide lumber, when houses and businesses increased as additional settlers arrived. Even by 1875, there were fewer than 200 inhabitants with 20 homes, a post office, a few shops, a school building and a little framed Presbyterian church. Then things changed quickly. The Pittsburgh, Shenango & Lake Erie Railroad now reached Pine Grove; a number of coal mines opened; Isaac Ketler was granted a charter for Pine Grove Normal School, now Grove City College; many local businesses were born; and the sleepy borough woke to the outer world. The name was changed in 1883 to Grove City because there was another Pine Grove Post Office in Pennsylvania. Soon it became a trading center and attracted people who came to make a permanent place of residence and business.

The 1900s continued Grove City's growth with Bessemer Gas Engine Co., founded by Dr. E.J. Fithian and John Carruthers (later merging with C.&G. Co. of Mt. Vernon , Ohio, to form Cooper-Bessemer Corporation), followed by the Volunteer Fire Company, grammar schools, a high school, the Grove City Hospital, banks, churches, George Junior Republic (a community for troubled youths), a new water plant, the government-built Creamery, Bashline Rossman Hospital (later a osteopathic medical school), Montgomery Builders Supply Co., the Penn Grove Hotel, Wendell August Forge, the George Howe Company and many more local businesses. In addition, the college was constantly expanding. Unlike Sharon, whose primary

A Montgomery Builders ad on September 16, 1941, in the Reporter-Herald boasted a ready supply of lumber.

The Department of Agriculture conducted experimental work on dairy products at the government-built Creamery from 1916 until it closed in 1948.

GROVE CITY, PA., TUESDAY, JULY 16, 1940

View of Grove City From 2500 Feet In The Air

Plans For Airport Here Enhanced By Developments

Youngsville Flying Instructor Seeks Location For School Here

Prospects for a suitable airport for Grove City were enhanced by a number of developments over the week end.

J. M. York of Youngsville, Pa., was in the city, seeking locations for a field where he might establish a flying school. He is a veteran flier, with 12 years of experience, and recently has been conducting a successful school at Youngsville. He was anxious to transfer his facilities to a location near a college, where CAA training might be developed for the students.

While here he contacted Dr. Dale Jamison of Saginaw, Michigan, who flies to Grove City frequently, and has been spending a short time here. The two took off and landed on several possible airport sites, and Mr. York expressed satisfaction with possibilities in several locations. It is probable that he will make definite commitments here within a short time.

Yesterday, Doctor Jamison flew for nearly an hour over the Grove City district, with F. H. Niece, A. J. Schell and David Shelley, of the Commercial Club aviation committee, and Floyd McClymonds.

(Continued On Page Six)

Above, airview of Grove City, taken yesterday by Dr. Dale Jamison from 2500 feet. The view is looking south. No. 1, top center, is the First Presbyterian Church. No. 2, at left, is the Cooper-Bessemer plant, and 3, right center, is the McKay Body Co.

At left, members of the aviation committee of the Commercial Club, F. H. Niece, A. J. Schell, David Shelley, and Floyd McClymonds.

The committee spent an hour over Grove City Monday, looking over possible sites. Several were found, including two or three that could be prepared at little expense. All were within three miles of Grove City.

By plane, the aviation committee looked for an airport site in Grove City in July of 1940, according to the Grove City Reporter-Herald.

employers were steel and other mills, Grove City now had a diverse base: dirty industry (the coal mines located outside city limits), semi-dirty but skilled industry (Cooper-Bessemer, nationally known for its large engines), small local businesses, a well-supported private college, and a hospital and medical school offering professional opportunities and a bit of culture.

The town had a history of entrepreneurs seeing potential opportunities for profit and going after them. As soon as FDR announced in '39 that a new CAA pilot training program would be started near colleges (and Grove City College had had the government's Student Army Training Program in 1918), a local airport was a must. The race was on. "Plans for Airport Here Enhanced By Developments" read headlines in the Reporter-Herald. On July 16, 1940, the Grove City Commercial Club's (a forerunner to the Grove City Area Chamber of Commerce) aviation committee flew over the city at 2,500 feet in a muscle Stinson piloted by Dr. Dale Jamison to identify potential sites. Jamison was working with J. M. York, a seasoned pilot with an existing flying school in Youngsville. York was "anxious to transfer his facilities to a location near (Grove City College). The committee and Jamison took off and landed on several locations, all within three miles of the business center. Any one of them could be improved to meet federal requirements with little expense. It is probable that York will make definite commitments here within a short time." This had turned into an adult game of hide and seek using airplanes, with the goal to find an airport site.

Since 1879, the McCoy farm property sat in Pine Township "beginning at a point in the center line of (the Grove City-Harrisville) road," a mile south of the center of Grove City off Route 173 (later called Airport Road). Several parcels were added over time, part being a 1.75-acre triangular parcel that the King Planing Mill and Supply Company sold in 1907 to King and Wilson, who in turn sold it in 1908 to McCoy and McClelland for $105. James Howard McCoy made brick molds by hand, carried clay from the Slippery Rock Creek running through the property, crafted an oven, then baked his bricks. He built his farmhouse and covered it with his handmade bricks and also constructed a wagon shed and barn. Findley and Maxine Wilson purchased 1.593 acres on March 24, 1941 (although it's possible they had already been leasing it and had the hangar built by then). Additionally at that time, Fin was leasing two other parcels from the McCoys that were used for runways. Fin purchased the next 56 acres in October of 1943 and a final 10 acres on January 12, 1944. The McCoys kept a 4.886 acre parcel with their house. The deed states "that the Wilsons will not disturb or destroy the drain from the cellar of the McCoys, that extends to a small stream (on Fin's newly purchased property), and the McCoys have the right to go onto the sold land to repair or replace the drain." He had mastered the tactics of leverage and negotiation. With faith in the future and in his abilities, he committed to buy the land with future income from the government CPTP contract. He owned it for 40 years, later leasing it to a national company on the stock exchange then finally selling it to a coal company for strip mining. Fin was a small man, but smart, cunning and nimble as a fox – a fox who had won the big race. Grove City now had an airport.

In a map of Grove City from the early 1990s, McCoy's farm property abuts Airport Road. The original McCoy farmhouse sits on 4.7 acres abutting the top left section of the 66-acre Baldeo property. The airport and its runways were on these 66 acres.

The date of this photograph of cadets marching at Grove City College is unknown, but staff members at the Air Force Historical Research Agency at Maxwell Air Force Base in Alabama believe it may be from the post-Civil War era, perhaps 1890-1911.

CHAPTER 3

The 8th Detachment and Grove City College

Grove City College was the dream and lifelong work of the Ketler and Pew families. While it is organically independent and controlled by a self-perpetuating Board of Trustees, it is loosely tied to the Presbyterian Church and committed to Christian principles. Its mission is to provide the highest quality education to families of modest means who desire a college that will strengthen their children's spiritual and moral character. Courses offered included liberal arts, humanities, science and engineering, music, fine arts, and later secretarial studies. Founder Isaac Ketler was President until 1913, and had grown enrollment from 13 to more than 660 students. Dr. Weir Ketler, Issac's son and a product of the school, took over leadership in 1916.

From the early 1890s until 1911, the College had a military sector that was sponsored by the War Department. All male students were expected to take part in a program of military training. An officer of the U.S. Army was detailed to direct and supervise the program. In 1917 on the entrance into World War I, Weir Ketler and the college organized, on its own initiative and at its own expense, a military training unit. In 1918, a unit of the Students Army Training Corps was organized with 235 cadets. This unit was in operation until after the signing of the Armistice.

In 1939, Grove City was chosen by the CAA as a cooperating school for the Civilian Pilot Training Program. It started small. Beginning in '40, the program was open to all students, and 10 were selected for the first class of both ground schooling and dual and solo flight training. Fin was awarded the flight school contract, leased the triangular piece from the McCoys and put up a rudimentary cement-block hangar. But it was all paid for. The college's aeronautics curriculum included 24 hours each in meteorology, navigation and civil air regulations, plus 18 hours in aircraft operation and a minimum of 35 hours flying time. This program was limited to 20, two of whom could be women. By October of '41, the CAA became more stringent and required a fully equipped airplane in each classroom in which the ground work curriculum was taught. Professor Russell Smith, ground instructor, installed an airplane in the third floor of the College Hall of Science. According to the local newspaper, "Instructors will invite all who are interested in aeronautics to visit the Science Hall to inspect the plane after the assemblage is completed. Improvements have been made on the hangar.

SELECTIVE SERVICE
LOCAL BOARD NO. 1
MERCER, MERCER CO. PA.
(STAMP OF LOCAL BOARD)

NOTICE TO REGISTRANT
TO APPEAR FOR
PHYSICAL EXAMINATION

August 29, 1941
(Date)

You are hereby directed to report to Dr. F. M. Bleakney
(Name of examining physician)
at Broad St. Grove City for physical examination at 2-4 P. m.,
(Address) 7-8 P. M.
on **or before September 4, 1941** Failure to do so is an act punishable by imprisonment and fine, and may also result in your losing valuable rights and in your immediate induction into military service.

Member of Local Board.

D. S. S. FORM No. 201

Selective Service ramps up as clouds of WWII approach the US.

Large doors have been put in place and preparations are being made for work on the interior (at the airport). Word has been received from Dave McGowan, who was last year's flight instructor, that he is now flying large army planes in Pensacola, Fla., and finds it slightly different from flying the Cubs back here in Grove City. Weather conditions have made solo flying impossible for the CAA students. It is expected that next week will make possible the first solo flights."

Grove City College's newspaper, The Collegian, stated on December 10, 1941 that, "The future of the CAA's course in Grove City College's is very uncertain, Prof. Russell Smith, ground instructor for the CAA, said today in conjunction with the announcement that the school's

CAA planes had been grounded Monday immediately following Pearl Harbor and declaration of war by the United States. Smith stated further that the war could mean a discontinuation of the course, while on the other hand, it may mean an enlargement of the course. Only time will tell. Authorities of the Findley Wilson Flying School, owners of the ships used by the student pilots, recalled all planes under their control to their base at New Castle, pending government orders concerning the permission to fly private planes. Speculation among authorities is that it is very possible that all private planes may be grounded for the duration to avoid identification of aircraft. Smith told the Collegian representative that letters have been received recently from former Grove

City CAA students who are now in the service of the United States military and naval divisions. They are enjoying their work but at the same time realize the seriousness of the task which lies ahead of them."

According to a December 1941 Collegian student newspaper, "Immediately after Pearl Harbor, the Trustees of Grove City College went on record, by resolution, authorizing the College Administration to lend its facilities and, so far as possible, to assist directly in the war effort." This might have been patriotic, but it was also pragmatic. In the years preceding the outbreak of the war, the normal attendance in the fall semester was over 900 students (500 men and 400 women). Male enrollment was dropping drastically, as was tuition income. Many male students, not only locally, but all over the United States left in droves to enlist in the Armed Forces. The Selective Service ruled to lower the draft age to 18 in November of '42. At one time there were only 40 civilian men enrolled at the school. The fate of the Civilian Pilot Training Program could make or break the shrinking cash flows.

The Alumni News reported in the spring of 1942 that, "after numerous delays and interruptions in the flight work due to drastic restrictions caused by the war, Grove City College completed the third CPT course during the fall semester. Fifty students have now taken the course and with a few exceptions have successfully completed both the flight work and the ground school. Forty-eight have passed the exams given by the government. Twenty more are currently enrolled. While civil flying has been greatly restricted due to war

One of the most popular courses at Grove City college is aviation, with keep competition for the ten places in the CAA class each semester. A new class is being formed to start Feb. 15. Prof. Russell P. Smith, ground school instructor, upper left, is explaining mechanical details of a ripped training plane. Standing, left to right, are Wellington Weidler, Oil City; James Frazer, New thlehem; William Black, Grove City; Don Kelly, Butler, and Tom Davies, Sharon. Kneeling ar Adams, Bellevue; Thomas Evens, Brentwood, and Brenton Holter, Grove City.

Professor Russell Smith brought a plane into his classroom at Grove City College in the fall of 1941. Kneeling is Brenton Holter.

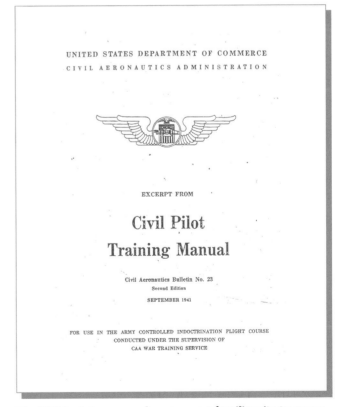

UNITED STATES DEPARTMENT OF COMMERCE

CIVIL AERONAUTICS ADMINISTRATION

EXCERPT FROM

Civil Pilot
Training Manual

Civil Aeronautics Bulletin No. 23
Second Edition
SEPTEMBER 1941

FOR USE IN THE ARMY CONTROLLED INDOCTRINATION FLIGHT COURSE
CONDUCTED UNDER THE SUPERVISION OF
CAA WAR TRAINING SERVICE

The CAA training manual cover was a familiar site to many.

Flying Course Is Popular With Students

In 1939, Grove City was chosen as a cooperating school for the Civilian Pilot Training Program of the Civil Aeronautics Authority. The program began in 1940, and consisted of both ground schooling and dual and solo flight training. The course was open to all interested students and about 10 were selected for the first course. From December, 1940 until June, 1941, the US Office of Education asked the college to offer an engineering defense training program. In 1940, the school's aeronautics curriculum included 24 hours each in meteorology, navigation, and civil air regulations, plus 18 hours in aircraft operation and a minimum of 35 hours flying time. This program was limited to twenty, two of whom could be women.

The Alumni News, a Grove City College publication in April 1942, referenced the continuation of the pilot training program.

Civilian Pilot Training Class Is Continued

Twenty Students Now Taking Course; 48 Have Passed Ground School Work

After numerous delays and interruptions in the flight work due to drastic restrictions caused by the war, Grove City College completed the third C.P.T. course during the fall semester. Fifty students have now taken the course and with a few exceptions, have successfully completed both the flight work and the ground school. Forty-eight of the fifty have passed the ground school examinations as given by the Government. Twenty more students are now taking the course, with the ground school more than half completed; a number have already soloed in their flight work.

While civil flying has been greatly restricted due to war regulations, we have been most fortunate in being able to continue our course. Mr. Wilson, the flight contractor, after constructing a modern hangar at the flying field, is constantly improving the condition of the field and the equipment of the hangar. An armed guard is on duty at the field at all times, and all planes taking off or arriving are required to register and are identified and examined. These precautions are necessary to eliminate the operation of any unidentified planes.

The spring program of the ground school has enrolled a number of students, not as C.A.A. students, but as college students taking the course to gain a knowledge of Meteorology and Navigation. At present there is an urgent demand for instructors in those particular fields and there are good opportunities for those able to pass the government examinations.

Grove City College has acquired equipment for the course this year, including a large globe for the study of navigation and a fully equipped plane which is installed in the aeronautics laboratory. It is hoped to add to this equipment as time goes on.

regulations, we have been most fortunate in being able to continue our course. Mr. Wilson is constantly improving the conditions of the field and the equipment of the hangar. An armed guard is on duty at the field at all times, and all planes taking off or arriving are required to register and are identified and examined. These precautions are necessary to eliminate the operation of any unidentified planes." Homeland Security is not a new phenomenon.

Future instructor Brenton Holter keeps in touch with his mom while in the Army Air Corps in '42.

The program at the college survived, but barely, and needed a dramatic shot in the arm. Current enrolled numbers didn't come close to producing enough income. On December 7, 1942, the name of the Civilian Pilot Training Program was changed to the War Training Service (WTS), along with a shift to war preparedness and all-out mobilization and centralized control by the military. The program was ramped up, with the WTS to continue to train enlisted reservists for pilot specialties. It would provide 10 hours of elementary flight instruction for the cadets who could then choose further training as a pilot, navigator, engineer or bombardier or enter gunnery school. All crewmen received this initial indoctrination training that prepared them to be able to fly a crippled plane back to base if the pilot was killed or injured during a mission. In December 1942, following a request received from the War Manpower Commission, a questionnaire was submitted giving information about Grove City College – its character, facilities, buildings, equipment and faculty. Earlier in March of '42, the college had opened a Naval School in basic radio. On February 3, 1943, a telegram was received from Maxwell Field, Ala., to the effect that a Board of Officers was en route to the college to make a survey to determine its availability to serve as a preparatory school for prospective aviation cadets. On February 6, 1943, a board of four, including two captains from Maxwell Field and two civilians, visited the college and made an inspection of the facilities there. Following their inspection, a telegram was received on February 9, 1943, signed by the Chief of the Air Staff, asking whether the college would accept a unit of

200 trainees. The first unit of 100 was to report on March 1, the second unit on April 1.

A letter of intent covering the contract for the unit was received in late February '43. Subsequently, on March 23, a contract committee visited the college, and further negotiations were carried on in the offices of the Army Air Corps in Detroit, Mich. Following this conference, Contract No. W 2119 ac-81 was prepared and signed by President Weir Ketler on June 14, 1943, only to be renegotiated and signed in final Contract W 30-053 ac-55 on August 16, 1943, well after the initial activation.

At 8 a.m. Sunday morning, February 28, 1943, the 8th College Training Detachment arrived in three buses from Atlantic City via Pittsburgh. The 90 enlisted men were mainly from the New England States. Now the college was training Marines, Navy cadets and the new Army Air Crew. And at the Cooper-Bessemer Diesel School were 80 men from the Coast Guard and Maritime Service, billeted in the barracks at Wendell August Forge, where men were also being trained in metal work. The town of Grove City had almost a complete military set-up.

Grove City College's third president Weir Ketler led from 1916-56 through two wars and the Depression.

The commandant was 1st Lt. Frederick E. Green, assisted by 2nd Lt. James Gialelis and 2nd Lt. Francis T. Stephens. The authorized strength of the 8th was 200 men. Dr. Weir Ketler appointed Dr. H.O. White the academic coordinator and 280

hours of academic and military training was set up, according to the Historical Station Report, "to prepare the air crew students, both mentally and physically, for intensive ground training in the preflight school" for becoming pilots, navigators or bombardiers. And these students obtained 10 additional hours of hands-on dual flight instruction at the airport. After arriving fully uniformed on Sunday and getting equipped, they were taken to Ketler Hall where they would be housed. Then their first activity as a unit was to march to Harbison Chapel for Sunday Vespers service. Early on Monday, March 1, the men of the 8th started on their intensive five-month course. Academic instruction came from the college faculty. Courses were taught stressing fundamentals first, then targeting war-related specifics.

Lt. Frederick Green headed the 8th College Training Detachment at Grove City College.

English, taught by Carl Easter and William Kirk, included military English, military vocabulary, nomenclature of aeronautics, the study of military correspondence and criticism as a military process rather than an artistic one.

Geography was covered by Daniel McEuen, Franklin Sumrall, Jonathan Ladd and James Mills and included topics ranging from the Earth, physical elements, the atmosphere, climatic data, maps, graphs, heating of the atmosphere, wind systems, atmospheric pressure and moisture to climate and weather in various war zones, region-

Harbison Chapel centered campus in the '40s, as it does now.

Cadets head to Harbison Chapel on the Grove City campus.

al geography, supplies and supply lines and the geography of Axis Strategy.

History and Americanism were taught by Levi Beeler and William Kirk. Lessons focused on the Old World and the New, WWI, the United States since 1918, the immediate background of this war (including brief study of all involved countries) and the new style of warfare.

Adam Kiefer and Carl Fink instructed on the mathematic principles of longitude and time; English to metric; conversion of nautical to statute; power vs. altitude of engines; vector and wind drift; time, ratio, and distance problems; and wind drift problems.

Physics and an ensuing physics lab was under the tutelage of Russell Smith, Philip Carpenter, Frank Ellis, Martin Radt and Edison Connor, who

spoke on falling bodies, projectiles (height attained, range, air resistance, bombs, gun fire, muzzle velocity), gases, the theory of flight, communication and Bernoulli's Principle, as well as CAA films on lift and drag, the airplane engine, wing forces, stability, air ocean, air masses, fuel and feed, and weather.

Esther Godwin Post taught medical aid and shared insight on the human body; the definition and study of wounds; shock; proven methods of applying hand and tourniquet pressure; punctured, infected and abdominal wounds; transporting wounds and fractures; improvised traction splints; burns and scalds (ordinary and chemical); sunstroke and exhaustion; poisons (food and gases); unconsciousness; and common emergencies.

Civil air regulations were instructed by

George Eggleston and Addison Leitch, who went over flight rules, specially designated areas, certification of pilots, aircraft certification, pilot regulations, miscellaneous regulations, emergency regulations and enforcement.

Physical training was supervised by the college athletic director Robert Thorn and included time in the indoor pool and weight room, basket shooting and chinning, calisthenics, medicine ball drills, relays, minor combatives, response drills, cross country running and obstacle courses.

Basic military indoctrination was conducted by officers and permanent party personnel under the direction and supervision of the Tactical Officer. These subjects included discipline and customs of service, interior guard and military hygiene and sanitation. There were other instructors mentioned in the 1944 Grove City College Ouija yearbook: Charles Ruffner, Roger Dawes, Samuel Yingst and Herbert Harmon – probable replacements for any of the above.

Mess was at 0730, 1230 and 1730 hours. All classes were held Monday through Friday, with drills or physical training late in the afternoon, remedial instruction or supervised study hall at 1900, followed by regular study hour from 2000 to 2100. On Saturday mornings, there was one hour of physical training for all cadets, as well as inspections, reviews and parades. WWII fighter pilot Bob Campbell, who enrolled in the CPTP program at the University of Toledo, recalls that "it was a rigorous academic program. The other half was phys. ed. with every imaginable type of sport: cross-country running in the snow over hills, football, wrestling, boxing. The endeavor was to make

vicious, bloodthirsty fighting men out of nice, young college kids with an interest in flying. We were ready to drop at the end of each day!"

The policy of Commanding Officer Green was that weekly tests were given by each academic instructor, and individual grades on each aviation student were submitted to the office of the 8th College Training Detachment. Based on these grades, weekend supervised study classes were held (including any student who received one or more grades below 70 percent). All aviation students on this list were not accorded Open Post for the weekend. Interior guard was maintained under Lt. Green's stay from 1900 to 0600, and guard posts extended about the barracks of the 8th Detachment. Guards did not carry rifles but were required to wear field helmets and carry clubs. At no time did the guards have any unusual or unmanageable experiences. The college and the Borough of Grove City embraced the cadets with friendliness and activities: two movie theaters, a roller skating rink, bowling alley, clean and pleasant restaurants, namely "The Diner." Directly across the street from the college, The Diner, opened in 1938, offered tasty and affordable food for the students, cadets and townspeople. A community service center, acting in the capacity of a U.S.O., provided dances, parties, refreshments, reading, letter writing and games. There were 12 churches that had open doors to the cadets. The Historical Station Report commented that, "The community as a whole had very high religious standards. And no instances or immorality or intemperance due to community activities were experienced. Grove City proper had an ordinance prohibiting the sale of liquor within the city limit."

According to the 1944 Ouija yearbook (chronicling the previous year), "The Air Cadets soon replaced the college boys who, until last year, helped make up the usual campus scene. The halls of Recitation Hall were crowded with boys and girls, but the boys were proudly wearing the uniform of the United States Army Air Corps instead of the usual sweaters, slacks and saddle shoes. The fellows and girls who were left on the campus welcomed these men wholeheartedly – for their own sakes as well as for the sake of the boys from Grove City who were Air Cadets on other campuses. Although we know that these boys are here to begin their preparation for a grim and serious business and we regret the circumstance that has forced them into uniform, we are glad to have had the opportunity to meet these men and hope that Grove City College will remain forever in their memories as a place where they made many friends and as a place where they spent several happy months. We know that they will remain in our memories as our friends and as a very important part of our college lives."

Air cadets and a few good Navy cadets gather outside of the Rockwell Hall of Science on the Grove City College campus.

The Grove City Airport flourished at the height of its Civilian Pilot Training Program days.

CHAPTER 4

Cadets, Cubs and Flight Training

One month after formal academic classes began, the first aviation students of the 8th College Training Detachment took their first flying lessons at Grove City Airport on April 1, 1943. By now, the 60-plus acres had two runways suitable for landing and taxiing; the north-south runway was 2,150 feet long and the east-west was 2,000 feet long. There was an expansive cement-block hangar suitable for housing all training planes stationed there and fitted with solid wide-paneled sliding doors. On the east end was a large ground school classroom on the first floor, with offices for administrative work above that. The west end of the hangar had an addition for an airplane repair and maintenance shop. Mounted on the roof with a substantial tripod was the trusted, dependable tubular wind sock. Two lines of trainer planes, mostly Piper Cubs, tied down in orderly fashion, waited out front for the eager cadets. Not only was the airport home to the 8th Detachment, but to the larger 329th Detachment out of Slippery Rock State College.

Administrative staff of the Grove City Airport included: owners/operators Findley and Maxine Wilson, New Castle, Pa.; manager Doris Smith (wife of physics professor Russell Smith), Grove City, Pa.; Chief Pilot Rufus "John" Tyndall, Grove City, Pa.; Assistant Chief Pilot Matthew Stormes, Grove City, Pa.; Assistant Chief Pilot Theodore Stage, Grove City, Pa.; CAA-War Training Service Resident Flight Supervisor Earl Platt Jr., Grove City, Pa.; and CAA-War Training Service Resident Maintenance Supervisor Julius Schaffer, Grove City, Pa. Flight instructors for the 8th College Training Detachment were Brenton Holter, Grove City, Pa.; Clarence Bell, Grove City, Pa.; Murl DeArment, Sharon, Pa.; Gardner Birch, Sharon, Pa.; and Theodore Stage, Youngstown, Ohio.

Flight instructors for the 8th Detachment cadets were, from left, Gardner Birch, Brenton Holter, Theodore Stage, Clarence Bell and Murl DeArment.

Instructors from both the Grove City and Slippery Rock detachments stand in front of an AAF twin-engine military plane. From left, Sol Liphinsky, Bill Heth, Jack Vernon, Ted Stage, Ed Horensky, Francis Bryan, Ray Flanagan, John Henderson, Seymour Heinberg, Frank Van Tassel, Fred Parsons, Gardner Birch, Chet Minnick and Brenton Holter. Instructors of diverse nationalities taught equally diverse cadets. This "mulligan stew" effort was a winning recipe for the CPTP.

Additional instructors at Grove City Airport were John Henderson, New Castle, Pa.; Sol Liphinsky; Joseph Burns, Youngstown, Ohio; Bill Heth; Joseph Marzlack, McKees Rocks, Pa.; Jack Vernon; Francis Masson, Sharon, Pa.; Ed Horensky; Fred Parsons; and Chet Minnick.

Other crucial cogs in the wheel that made the airport run were A&E Certified Licensed Mechanic Alex Hogg, Erie, Pa.; three mechanic helpers; three or more line boys, teenagers Ellis Klingensmith, Bill "Willie" Raymer and Ray Cornelius, Grove City, Pa.; secretaries Jeanne Carruthers, Margaret Fithian, Rosie Rowe and Mrs. Heater.

Airport office staff included, from left, manager Francis Masson, Rosie Rowe, Nancy Smith, Doris Smith and Mrs. Heater.

Flight instructors for the 329th Detachment from Slippery Rock State College, were, from left, seated, Lou Caramella and Walter Wiewel; standing, Ray Flanagan, Elliott Jones, Frank Van Tassel, Richard Reed, Francis 'Doc' Bryan, Durward 'Dud' Canfield, John Subject, Seymour Heinberg, Bill Cooper, Benjamin Baker and Roscoe Harris.

Flight Instructors for the 329th Detachment from Slippery Rock included Louis Caramella of East Stroudsburg, Pa., an athlete at Lehigh University and a former football and basketball coach; Walter Wiewel, Jr., a student at Shadyside Academy, Aspinwall, Pa.; Raymond Flanagan of Rutland, Vt., a redheaded basketball playing Irishman who studied piano and organ at McGill Conservatory in Montreal; Elliott "Buck" Jones of Sharon, Pa., who studied law at the University of Pittsburgh and was a reporter and newscaster; Frank "Wolf" Van Tassel of Grove City, Pa., who instructed students in his own Piper Cruiser; Richard Reed, Altoona, Pa., recently married and an instructor at West Point; Francis "Doc" Bryan, who received flight training from five different colleges; Durward "Dud" Canfield, Mayville, N.Y., a former motorcycle daredevil and test crash

driver; John Subject, Olean, N.Y., a father of two who took his first parachute jump in 1930; Seymour Heinberg of New York, N.Y., who earned a bachelor's degree from City College, was a CPA and also newly married; Bill Cooper, Youngstown, Ohio, who attended Pitt, where classmates claimed "he would hock his clothes to pay for an airplane ride"; Benjamin Baker of Brooklyn N.Y., a former machinist instructor at Brooklyn Navy Yard who had his own flying service and was a big Dodgers fan; and Roscoe Harris of State College, Pa., an auto mechanic who received CPTP training from Randolph Field, Texas.

Fin's hometown business success was now about 15 years in the making. And it was very much tied to another, but much larger Pennsylvania entrepreneurial success story – the quiet, legendary man who pioneered a generation of small airplanes for hundreds of thousands of pilots and made "Bill Piper" and "Cub" synonymous with those ubiquitous yellow two-seaters. His $400 investment over the next 30 years would grow to $30 million.

Bill Piper was living in Bradford, Pa., in the late 1920s running his family's oil business. Gilbert Taylor was looking for a place to locate his Taylor Brothers aircraft factory. Piper invested $400 and was quickly pushed onto the aircraft company's board. He and Taylor clashed quickly over product strategy; Taylor had priced his "Chummy" at $4,000, Piper wanted an airplane people would find easy to buy, easy to fly and easy on the wallet. As the two men struggled, so did the company, and Taylor declared bankruptcy in 1930. Because of the Depression, no one bid on the assets, so Piper bought them for $761 and gave back half interest to Taylor.

In 1932, Piper hired a 19-year-old who claimed to be an aeronautical engineer and who was willing to work for free. Walter Jamouneau made slight changes to a newly designed Cub, including rounded wing tips, a curved rudder and fin, a true cabin and an enclosed cockpit. When the altered Cub rolled out of the factory, it became the J-2. The price then, and for years to come, was $1,325. In 1937, a devastating fire forced relocation to Lock Haven, Pa. An empty silk mill next to the Lock Haven Airport and railroad line had more space than the Pipers ever thought they would need. But it later turned into a trump card. They convinced military brass that the small plane could perform special duties in war, and their

rebuilt plant was the only one with enough capacity to produce the needed quantities, many for instructing cadets being trained in the CPTP.

Teaching people to fly meant additional aircraft sales. Dealers and distributors could send to Lock Haven any youth who wanted to learn to fly. The students paid their transportation, lodging and meals, and Piper taught them to fly for $1 an hour, which included the airplane and the instructor. The same low cost applied to employees. In 1934, plant workers received 20 cents an hour, and scores took advantage of the $1-an-hour training. "The best part of this," recalled Bill Piper Jr., "is that so long as the kids wanted to fly they would be interested in building a good product." At one time, one out of every 90 people in Lock Haven held a pilot's license. Jamouneau now had room to implement more changes that gave birth in 1938 to the J-3 Cub.

Simple and basic are the tenets of the Piper J-3: a welded steel tubing frame for fuselage and wings, covered with cloth, with a single engine (40 to 65 horsepower) exposed on the nose behind a wooden propeller. No starter or key, no electrical system, no radio and no blind flying instrumentation. Prop the plane and the engine starts. The Cub was 6 feet and 8 inches high, 22 feet long and weighed 680 pounds with a wingspan of just over 35 feet. The landing gear had a front split axle with shock absorber, two low-pressure tires and hydraulic brakes. A steerable tail wheel supported the weight of the tail end and allowed landing on rough terrain, hence the name "tail dragger." The enclosed cockpit, entered by the right-side door, had two tandem seats. The front was 14 inches wide; the back was 24 inches wide with dual control sticks and dual rudder pedals with cable attachments and heel brakes. A throttle, fuel shut-off and stabilizer control were on the left-side wall of each tandem seat for control by student, teacher or both. The ignition switch was on the left side of the ceiling and the carburetor heater control was on the right side of cockpit. The instrument panel was also basic: an airspeed indicator, an altimeter, tachometer, fuel primer and magnetic compass. The 12-gallon gas tank sat in front of the panel in the fuselage. With a 65-horsepower Continental, Lycoming or Franklin engine, the J-3 Cub could attain a maximum speed of 85 miles per hour with a ceiling of 9,300 feet. Those 12 gallons of gasoline were sufficient to fly about 190 miles. The nose of this tail dragger sat high on ground, thus the pilot could not see ground level out the front window while on land. While taxiing for take-off, the pilot had to fishtail the nose to make sure all was clear in front. Once airborne and leveled out, the pilot could clearly see out the front window a new world made possible by the simple Cub.

The additional factory space turned out to be a gold mine for the Pipers. The J-3 was now the basic trainer for four out of every five pilots in World War II and the CPTP's primary civilian-owned trainer. "All we had to do," recalled Bill Piper Jr., "was paint the Cub olive drab to produce a military airplane, a version called the L-4." In the four years spanning 1942-1945, Piper delivered 6,028 aircraft to the military. The uses were many. An umpire of war games discovered he could use the small planes to oversee the maneuvers. A commander of a column of tanks went

The Civilian Pilot Training Program's most important trainer – the Piper J-3 Cub. This is N88422, its U.S. civil aircraft registration number. The manufacturer assigns an 'N' number to a new plane and it is registered by the first owner with the FAA. That number stays with a plane its entire life.

The instrument panel in a J-3, from left, a tachometer, airspeed indicator, magnetic compass, altimeter, oil temperature and pressure gauge. The knob at the far left is for cabin heat and the knob on right is the engine primer.

aloft to untangle a massive traffic jam; flying low over the tangled mass, he bellowed instructions from a bullhorn. Pilots learned to avoid fighter planes by flying low and slow or by putting the L-4 into a tight spin while the attacking fighters raced past them. During the Italian campaign, L-4s took off from converted LSTs (Landing Ship Tanks) and scouted the shorelines, far enough out to avoid small-arms fire. By putting a turtle top on the fuselage to increase headroom, the L-4 became a stretcher carrier. It supplied ground troops by dropping food, water, ammunition and blood plasma during the Battle of the Bulge.

The enemy quickly recognized the effectiveness of the "Grasshoppers," as the military Cubs were called. German fighter pilots received twice as many points toward an air medal for shooting down a Grasshopper rather than a fighter plane. Ground force personnel were promised a 15-day pass if they destroyed an observation plane. But the sales boom for private aircraft deflated as quickly as it had expanded. By 1948, many of Pipers' competitors had quit the field. By 1947, when production ended, 14,125 Piper J–3 Cubs had been built in nine years. Of that number, more than 5,500 remain on the FAA's aircraft registry today. The Aircraft Owners and Pilots Association (AOPA), America's leading general aviation organization, featured the J–3 in its October 2005 magazine and put its production into great perspective. "Cirrus Design, a general aviation aircraft company doing well by modern standards, just delivered its 2000th SR-series airplane in June of 2005, nearly seven years into its manufacturing run. Some longevous Cubs are now nearly 70 years young and still purring like kittens." Jack Lakeman, who bought his "Super" J–3 in 1970 from Marion Cole (head of the famed Cole clan of aerobatic pilots) and still owns it, authored this truism, "To the uninitiated, you can't explain it: to those who know, no explanation is necessary." Cubs are time machines: they bring people into flying and keep generations connected.

For example, the late Robert Stewart of Erie bought his first J-2 in 1936. His granddaughter, April Stewart, a graduate student at Carnegie Mellon University, soloed in that airplane in 1998 at Lock Haven's annual Sentimental Journey. The family, with deep aviation ties, devotedly flies back yearly to the event.

Back at Grove City Airport, the 8th Detachment and its five instructors had six of those J-3 Cubs and a Taylorcraft DC-65 for flight instruction. They were between three and six years old and the average number of flying hours per plane was less than 70 hours. The 329th Detachment had more than double that number. The government had stringent rules and procedures that were followed to the letter. All training planes had to be hangared each night. The line boys brought them in, tipped them tail-up and nose to the floor and put wooden blocks under the prop (or propeller) to hold the plane in a stable position. It was like packing pickles into a jar to get all the planes inside each evening. In the morning, these young guys reversed each step: they removed the blocks, righted the crafts and wheeled them onto the grass runway in two lines – the Slippery Rock line and the Grove City line. Line boys also filled gas tanks, washed the aircraft and propped the planes.

Ellis Klingensmith, now 80 and living in Ashtabula, Ohio, has a sharp memory of those days as a 17-year-old line boy living in Grove City. "Each instructor was assigned to a plane. All had their own distinction, but the 'darling' of the time was the Continental 65. Lycoming and Franklin had been favorites before that. There was one plane with a 50-horsepower engine, and no one wanted it. The instructor sat in the front seat in front of the instrument panel and the student in

CLOCKWISE FROM ABOVE: Gardner Birch, Murl DeArment, Clarence Bell and Brenton Holter, four key instructors in the Civilian Pilot Training Program in Grove City, Pa. BELOW: 17-year-old Ellis Klingensmith, far left, leans against a Piper J-3 Cub with two other line boys in 1943.

the larger rear seat, both with dual controls. Then, standing out in front near the prop, I would always give the same command, 'Gas on, switch off, throttle cracked.' That was their reminder to turn the gas valve on, make sure the magneto switch was off and open up the throttle a little. They would act and repeat back, 'Gas on, switch off, throttle cracked.' Next I would pull the prop through the compression stroke, maybe two or three times, and call, 'Brakes and contact' (meaning engage the brake pedals and make contact). They would step on the brake pedals and turn both magneto switches on and repeat, 'Brakes and contact.' Then I would pull the prop through. Hopefully the engine would start!"

Propping the plane is not without danger. Ellis says, "Today a 17-year-old would probably not be allowed to perform that task." No matter how many times line boys propped a plane, the

fact remained that they were very much a whirling cleaver and were always encouraged to remember to be wary of a temperamental engine that will start when least expected.

Maintenance on the airplanes was strictly observed per government directives. Prior to the day's flight operation, each plane had a compulsory inspection. Oil was changed after every 25 hours of flying. Every plane was given a 100- and 500-hour inspection and necessary overhaul. All major overhauls were accomplished in accord with manufacturer's specifications. Fire control materials were maintained in accordance with existing CAA regulations. Thirteen parachutes were assigned to the aviation students of the 8th Detachment. Parachutes were required for any aerobatics, and spins and snap rolls were considered as such. These parachutes were stored in open wooden bins in normally heated rooms and were repacked every 60 days according to CAA regulations. Instruction on the use of the parachutes and conditions warranting "bailing out" was given to all aviation students before flying. There was adequate first aid emergency equipment, including a crash truck.

Jeanne (Davidson) Carruthers and Margaret (Bovard) Fithian, both Grove City College students, worked as secretaries at the airport during the CPTP. Francis Masson was the overall airport manager for Fin, and Mrs. Russell Smith, whose husband was the physics professor at the college, was the office manager. The Smiths often provided the young women rides to the airport since gasoline was still rationed. Jeanne's grandfather, John Carruthers, and Margaret's uncle, Dr. E.J.

A small carryout on the McCoy farm sold lunch and pie to cadets. The airport sat directly behind it on cleared land.

Fithian, along with Jack McCune, founded the Bessemer Gas Engine Company in 1898. In 1928, they sold it and each received a million dollars in cash. Jeanne, on the other hand, worked at the airport after college graduation for $18 per week. Her prime responsibility was tracking the flying time for each plane so that the proper maintenance could be preformed. One of Jeanne's fondest memories was the small carryout located in a shed-type structure on the McCoy farm. Lunch and pie was sold each day to many hungry cadets. Jeanne recalls that when it was her turn to buy for the office, everyone ordered pie and coffee. But when someone else was paying, she only got coffee. Her mouth still waters over the delicious banana cream pie.

Margaret relates that "at 21 years old, I didn't take my job too seriously, but I took it because I didn't feel I should be loafing during World War II. The airport was closed on Sundays, but for security reasons, someone always had to be on duty. I was on duty one Sunday, when all of a sudden I heard a plane sputtering, trying to land on the grass runway. A Navy dive-bomber from Massachusetts was flying to Emlenton, Pa., and was 10 minutes from running out of gasoline. It finally hit the swamp area, and flipped on its wings, which were demolished. I ran to the telephone and cranked it so hard I almost electrocuted myself with the cranking! I finally reached military security at the college, told them about the crash and pleaded to send someone immediately. I also called the State Police." Grabbing the fire extinguisher, she went running toward the crash, climbed over a barbed wire fence and reached the

Headquarters for the 8th Detachment were home to many.

Cadets settle into a new life. As Lt. Stephens said, 'Nearly all the men who were assigned to this detachment as aviation students were raw recruits with only a few weeks basic training. These men were from all walks of life: lawyers, engineers, farmers and just plain kids.'

pilot who had broken his shoulder. On that fateful Sunday afternoon, Margaret rose to the occasion and took her job very seriously.

With quality equipment and support staff in place, all that was needed for training success were competent cadets and instructors. Francis Stephens documents, "Nearly all the men who were assigned to this detachment as aviation students were raw recruits with only a few weeks basic training. These men were from all walks of life: lawyers, engineers, farmers and just plain kids. An attempt was made to weld these men into one composite unit so that a man with little or no educational, social or business background could not be differentiated from those who had been more fortunate prior to entering the armed services. Regardless of nationality or creed, immediately upon entering this detachment all distinguishing marks of assimilated or actual superiority or inferiority were discarded. Each man was equal with the same privileges and rights as any other."

When the instructors began teaching on April 1, 1943, they were the mirror of their students in composite and only one step up the ladder in

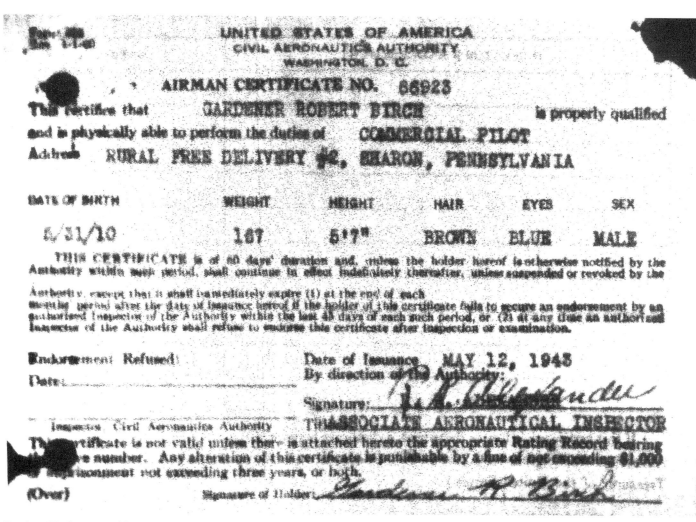

Gardner Birch received his commercial pilot's certification, which was necessary to teach in the Civilian Pilot Training Program, on May 12, 1943.

training. The 8th Detachment cadets would end up with 10 hours in the sky, while the instructors began with less than 300. This was their golden opportunity to fast-forward their flight hours, with no cost to them, and receive a pay check of $250 per month for doing something they loved. It equates to Dick Vitale covering March Madness for ESPN and rasping in wonderment, "And we get PAID for this? I'd do it for free!"

Flight instruction time for cadets, who would get 10 hours of dual flight time (probably just Stage A/see Box 4B), was scheduled into at least 58 flying days. Each instructor had eight students per day but could not exceed a 36-hour week. The basis for ground school class work was Civil Aeronautics Bulletin No. 32, titled "Fundamentals of Elementary Flight Maneuvers." Pre-flight ground school was held prior to actual flying in the ground level classroom. Daily ground instruction in proportion of one-half to one of flight instruction was given before and after each flight. The outline of the original, longer four-stage program (a minimum outline), follows as per CAA procedure bulletin (June 4, 1940).

The CAA recommended "that flight trainees arrive at the airport 10 minutes before reporting to the flight instructor. They should sign in and ready parachutes and equipment for a 45-minute period with the flight instructor. They should have an extra five minutes after their 15 minutes of ground instruction and half-hour flight time to replace equipment, sign logbook or any necessary papers. This should result in a smooth running schedule of six hours per flight instructor per day.

Clarence E. Bell
RFD # 2, Emlenton, Pa.

Gardener R. Birch
RD # 2, Sharon, Pa.

Murl E. DeArment
518 Wilson St.
Sharon, Pa.

Brenton B. Holter
RD # 4, Grove City, Pa.

C. Theodore Stage
1059 Hawthorne St.
Youngstown, Ohio

Matthew A. Stormes
219 E. Smith St.
Corry, Pa.

Rufus B. Tyndall
222 College Ave.
Grove City, Pa.

Francis W. Bryan
80 Western Ave.
Westfield, Mass.

William P. Cooper, Jr.
60 Shadyside Drive
Youngstown, Ohio

Joseph Burns
884½ Rose St.
Youngstown, Ohio

Raymond B. Flanagan
83 Meadow St.
Rutland, Vermont — *Rutland, Vt.*

Roscoe E. Harris
RFD # 1, ~~State College~~, Pa.
Port Matilda, Pa.

Seymour Heinberg
1645 Gr. Concourse
New York, New York

Elliott R. Jones
417 Spruce Ave.
Sharon, Pa.

John F. Henderson
306 Lincoln Ave.
New Castle, Pa.

Joseph E. Marzlack
1150 11th St.
McKees Rocks, Pa.

Francis Masson
277 McClure Ave.
Sharon, Pa.

Richard E. Reed
211 S. 2nd. St.
Altoona, Pa.

John M. Subjeck
1020 Walnut St.
Olean, New York

R. Frank Van Tassel
65 E. Frederick St.
Corry, Pa.

Walter H. Wiewel, Jr.
1060 Morewood Ave.
Pittsburgh, Pa.

*Jeanne Carruthers
Washington Blvd.
Grove City, Pa.*

The instructor's list typed by typewriter on onion skin paper. Jeanne Carruther's name is written by hand.

'All work and no play' might possibly get some of our flight instructors into some tight places as naturally there is a slowing down of reflexes when we are physically tired. Two suggested remedies are: take a regular day off—and always the same day; and have early morning flight training, mid-day rest, and resume in late afternoon."

Safety had top priority. Even with rules and regulations, checks and balance systems and inspections, there was the human factor. Many of the cadets were not adults, but still teenagers living out a dream and feeling invincible. And many

Box 4B

This is an outline of the original four-stage program of instruction. It comes from the CAA procedure bulletin (June 4, 1940).

STAGE A. DUAL INSTRUCTION

(minimum 8 hours)

a. Familiarization with airplane
b. Simple explanation of controls
c. Simple explanation of instruments
d. Explanation of throttle
e. Explanation of brakes
f. Explanation of fuel system
g. Use of safety belts
h. Location of fire extinguisher
i. Location of first-aid kit
j. Warnings
  (1) Propeller danger
  (2) Running engine with empty cockpit
  (3) Local traffic rules
k. Instruction signals

ADDITIONAL GROUND INSTRUCTION (to be given before solo)

a. Starting procedure
b. Swinging propeller
c. Warming up engine
d. Stopping engine
e. Line inspection of plane
f. Use of parachutes

Note: Instruction periods should be 30 minutes each, not more than two periods a day, with at least two hours of rest between periods. Students should be permitted to solo at any time after eight hours when, in the opinion of their instructors, they are qualified. The order of teaching and time spent on the following maneuvers is left to the instructor's judgment to suit his conditions and personnel.

I. TAXIING TO PROFICIENCY (to be given with daily instruction throughout dual periods while taxiing from line to point of take-off and from point of landing to line)

a. Into wind
b. Crosswind
c. Down wind
d. Gusty wind

II. AIR WORK

a. Straight and level flight
b. Turns—medium-precision—to be introduced as soon as possible
c. Coordination exercises: 'S' turns, elementary 8s
d. Confidence maneuver
e. Normal climbs and glides
f. Turns in climbs and glides including 'S' patterns
g. Rectangular course around ground object—right and left
h. Stalls from level flight and turns
i. Steep power turns—right and left

III. TAKE-OFFS (explanation of difference between ground and air speed; effect of wind velocity and directions)

a. Into wind
b. Crosswind (demonstrate)

IV. LANDINGS (using 90- and 180-degree approaches; explain key positions)

a. Into wind
b. Crosswind (demonstrate)

V. SPINS (never to exceed two turns)

a. Normal entry and recovery
b. Accidental spins—demonstrations of inadvertent entries from climbing turns, steep turns (both with and without power) and from skidding turns; student to be shown what is meant by "cross-controls" and warned to avoid such use

VI. SIMULATED FORCED LANDINGS (emphasis placed on right approaches)

a. On take-off with less than 200 feet of altitude
b. 90 degrees with over 200 feet of altitude
c. 180 degrees above 400 feet of altitude—to be given on all periods after landing practice has commenced

STAGE B. PRIMARY SOLO

(minimum 3 hours solo—one-hour check to be given as instructor deems necessary)

Note: Instruction and solo periods should be 30 minutes each, not more than two periods in any one day, with at least two hours rest between periods. Check periods may be shortened. One dual check flight of all maneuvers in Stage A should be given.

VII. SOLO FLIGHT

VIII. SOLO PRACTICE—Work of Stage A periods I, II (except d, h, i), III, IV only; all take-offs and landings into wind only; all landing practice without power.

STAGE C-1. PRECISION MANEUVERS

(minimum 7 solo hours—4 dual)

Note: Instruction and solo periods should be 30 minutes to one hour, final discretion left to the instructor after judging student and his tendency to tire, but not more than two periods in one day, with at least two hours rest between periods.

IX. Instruction (1 hour) / Solo practice (2 hours)

a. Precision landings (180-degree side approach, altitude not to exceed 1,000 feet)
b. 30-degree eights around pylons (altitude 500 feet—maximum starting bank 30 degrees)

X. Instruction (1 hour) / Solo Practice (1 hour)

a. Review period IX
b. Stalls
c. Spins

XI. Instruction (1 hour) / Solo Practice (2 hours)

a. Review period X
c. Precision landings (360 degrees overhead approach—altitude not to exceed 1,500 feet)
c. 70-degree power turns (720-degree precision)

XII. Instruction (1 hour) / Solo Practice (2 hours)

a. Review period XI
b. Precision landings (spiral approach—minimum two turns—altitude not to exceed 2,000 feet)
c. 70-degree eights around pylons (altitude 800 feet—minimum starting bank 70 degrees)

STAGE C-2. CROSS COUNTRY AND FINAL REVIEW (minimum 8 hours solo, 4hours dual)

Note: Instruction and solo periods should range be 30 minutes to one hour, except period XV, which may be extended. Final discretion is left to the instructor in each case but not more than two periods should be given in one day, with at least two hours rest between periods.

XIII. Instruction (1 hour) / Solo Practice (2 hours)

a. Review period XII
b. Crosswind take-offs and landings
c. Slips (forward and side)

XIV. Instruction (1 hour) / Solo Practice (1 hour)

a. Review period XIII
b. Power approaches and power landings
c. "Dragging" fields (instruction only)

XV. Instruction (1 hour) / Solo Practice (2 hours)

a. Review period XIV
b. Cross country
c. Solo cross country 50 miles minimum and two full-stop landings at different airports—triangular course

XVI. Instruction, solo practice as needed. Complete private flight test given by instructor, and student goes through two complete tests alone and practices maneuvers.

XVII. Check by Instructor for Private Flight Test.

Number of Hours

Stage	Dual	Solo
A. Dual	8	
B. Primary solo	1	5
C. Advanced solo	8	13
TOTAL	**17**	**18**

of the instructors were only in their 20s, possibly short on the experience and maturity that only comes with age. A CAA Special Standing Notice in the summer of 1940 asking for "tightening up of supervision" notes two fatal accidents. "Both fatalities are directly chargeable to VIOLATIONS of the controlled flight course. One fatality occurred when a flight trainee, instructed to practice rectangular courses plus landings and take-offs, 'wandered' 10 miles away from the airport. Said flight trainee was next seen flying low and circling the home of a relative. The usual wave to a girlfriend — stalled airplane — too low for recovery — and another black mark for aviation, not to mention the loss of a flight trainee who might yet be with us had original instructions been adhered

to. Number two fatality concerned a flight trainee who insisted on practicing solo spins – WITHOUT A PARACHUTE – and against orders of flight instructor. This special notice, directed to Flight Operators and Flight Instructors, ended with 'You have the authority—the responsibility—take over the supervision—demand compliance and thus command respect!'"

Only one accident occurred at the Grove City Airport during the Civilian Pilot Training Program. It was due to engine failure. On April 10, 1943, a cadet and instructor Brenton Holter made a forced landing in a Piper Cub in a mead-

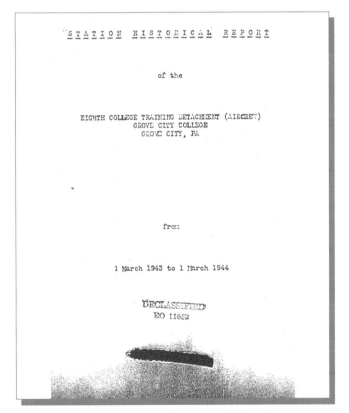

The Station Historical Report from the 8th Detachment at Grove city College was written by Commanding Officer Francis T. Stephens.

Photographs documented the plane crash of Brenton Holter and one of his students. The student sustained minor injuries while the injuries to the Piper Cub were major.

329th C.T.D.

Vol. 2   TUESDAY, NOVEMBER 30, 1943   NO. 5

New Top Men Are Appointed

Student Officers And Group Staff Are Announced

On Saturday, November 20, a new group Staff took over the command of the 329th C. T. D.

Assigned to the post of Group Commander, replacing T. G. Davis, is Thomas F. Hines, former "B" Squadron Commander. Tom was born in Stuart, Florida, where he lived the first five years of his life before moving to Montana. He lived in Montana for two years, at the end of which time he made Spottsylvania, Virginia, his new and present home. Upon graduation from high school, Tom attended V. P. I. where he was on the football varsity, and served in the R. O. T. C. He enlisted in the cadets early in 1943 and was called into active service in July. After taking Basic Training at Greensboro, N. C. he was shipped to the 329th.

Our new Adjutant, replacing

Flight Instructors for Slippery Rock Squadrons

Above are the men who have been brave enough to step forward and undertake the serious business of

The November 30, 1943, edition of the Flyin' Rapier, the newspaper of the 329th Aircrew based at Slippery Rock State Teachers College, featured a story on student officers and flight instructors.

ow 1.5 miles north of Harrisville under difficult conditions with a high wind blowing. The results for the trainee were: wound, severely lacerated right forehead and a mild contusion to the lower back. Results on the plane – extensive damage. The Contract Surgeon administrated necessary medial attention, and the aviation student was hospitalized in the 8th College Training Detachment hospital until fully recovered.

The 329th published a regular newspaper called the "Flyin' Rapier" (the rapier being a

straight two-edged sword with a narrow pointed blade). It reported on November 30, 1943, that "One of our boys, Clark 'Crash' Hines, had the first crack up at Wilson Airport. It seemed that while in the procedure of taxiing for a take-off, he hit a mud hole and piled up the plane. Damages slight, only a broken prop and no bodily injuries."

On August 31, 1943, a Captain and 2nd Lieutenant from the Army Air Force, Air Inspection Section of Maxwell Field, Ala., made an inspection of the flying facilities of Grove City

A cartoon in the November 30, 1943, edition of the Flyin' Rapier brought a light moment to pilots and cadets.

Airport. Their recommendations are: "The contractor (Fin) stated that at present he was not allowed to use airplanes from one school's program on the other school. It is recommended that the contractor be allowed to use all airplanes assigned as he may see fit." They were satisfied with the size and condition of the airfield, the parking area, the "very satisfactory" flying instruction, logs and progress charts being in order and the clean and orderly hangar. The Grove City Airport and Wilson Aviation Company received a commendation from District CAA Flight Supervisor James McClure on November 25, 1943, for having the best record of safety in the district.

Seymour Heinberg, an instructor for the 329th Detachment at Slippery Rock State College, pilots a plane, most likely a Stinson SR-9.

CHAPTER 5

A Day in the Life of a CPTP Cadet

The cadet's life at Grove City College was full – possibly too full. The detachment cooperated with the college and community in various patriotic and community affairs when requested. On Memorial Day of 1943, a chosen group of well-trained aviation students performed in a community parade. On Flag Day, June 14, 1943, they cooperated with the Elks Club in celebrating the occasion. On Armistice Day, along with the American Legion, cadets presented a 15-minute program as part of the Armistice Day commemoration in the auditorium of the college. On several other occasions, officers of the detachment made public appearances at the Kiwanis Club, American Legion meetings, Boy Scout rallies and high school programs, giving orientation talks concerning the Air Corp Training Program.

Under the direction of Professor Oscar Cooper, a college music instructor, an aviation student glee club was formed. Members gave regular performances at local churches, the college chapel, the college radio station and civic functions. The 8th Detachment also took an active participation in the 3rd and 4th War Bond Drives. Approximately 75 percent of all military person-

nel at this station were subscribers under the Class "B" allotment plan. In the 3rd War Bond Drive, $10,168.75 in case sales of bonds were made to military personnel and $150 to civilian personnel. In the 4th War Bond Drive, $2,762.45 were made to military personnel and another $150 went to civilian personnel.

The student body of the college extended invitations to the cadets and their guests to attend all events of interest: dances, plays, concerts and religious activities. Every effort was made by the students to make the young aviators students feel at home. During this period, however, Commanding Officer Green sponsored only one dance for his men, even though there was recreational fund money available for entertainment.

Six miles to the south, College President John Entz was a strong leader at Slippery Rock State College, a four-year teachers college on 600 historic acres. Slippery Rock's larger 329th Detachment trained at Grove City Airport and was headed by Capt. Llewellyn Werner. Bea "Beatrice" Rosenthal Heinberg, born, raised and still living in New York City, was a 20-year-old war bride when she joined her Slippery Rock instructor husband, Seymour, in Grove City in

Slippery Rock Air Cadets entertained in East Gymnasium in early 1944.

1943. They settled in Mrs. Albright's house, and Bea fondly remembers "experiencing some culture shock adjusting to this sleepy little town, especially on Sundays when everything was closed. The only thing to do was to walk to Isaly's for an ice cream cone. But I loved the town. One winter we were asked to chaperone a cadet dance in Slippery Rock at the college (she recalls the nickname 'Slimy Pebble'). There was a terrible snow storm that night on the way home, and another instructor had to walk outside the car and hold a flashlight, while Seymour, who was driving, searched for the road in blizzard conditions. Another time, on a Saturday, someone brought a new plane into the airport that had not been checked out. Seymour was home for lunch when

he got a call from Doc Bryan and Roscoe Harris. They asked him if he wanted to go on the 'check out.' He said to me, 'Bye, I don't know when I'll be back.' That evening I visited a friend who worked at Cooper-Bessemer and, because it was dark, he walked me home. I still had not heard from Seymour. Finally at 3 a.m., I was frantic and called the house where some of the younger Slippery Rock instructors lived. 'Japanese Embassy' was how they answered (the phone), but after I explained who was calling, I learned that after the 'check out' the guys had flown to State College so that Roscoe 'could pick up his car that was there to be fixed.' Seymour got home at 5 or 6 a.m. After the CPTP he was called to active duty and was released in November of 1945. He came back to

New York City and became a CPA for all his life, passing in 2003."

The Slippery Rock cadets had a dance saluting the upperclassmen of Squadron A, according to the the 329th Detachment's monthly newspaper, the "Flyin' Rapier." That November 30, 1943, edition reported that "Babe" Rhodes and his popular dance band let out with the notes on November 19. Billy Brent, the Man of Merriment, pounded on the skins in the style of Gene Krupa, while the band set forth some rhythmic rumba numbers. Babe had quite a reputation in Pittsburgh; his was the staff orchestra for the WCAE radio station.

Roscoe Harris, Seymour's roommate and Slippery Rock instructor, was born in Bellefonte, Pa., and learned to fly at Stulz Field in Tipton, Pa. The field, later known as Peterson Memorial, was operated by Wilmer Stulz, Amelia Earhart's pilot on her transatlantic passenger flight. In December 1944, after his instructor days at Grove City, Harris married Louise Daniels and joined the Air Force as an Air Transport Commandant until WWII ended. Louise, now 87 and living in Charlotte, N.C., says, "Roscoe loved that group in Grove City. After the war, he continued to instruct on the side while working at a car dealership, but he hated that. He made so many aware of flying, and always loved it! Finally a pilot's job came along: first with Tom Davis at Piedmont Aviation, then with H. L. Coble Construction Company of Greenville for 10 years. Then he went with Air Services, Inc. and sold Beechcraft airplanes. He was sales manager in Greenville until he died in 1983 of a heart attack."

The "Flyin' Rapier," again in its November 30, 1943, edition, had an anonymously written "student of the week column," spotlighting Joseph Truskolowski.

"If one only looks around and asks a few questions of some of the men at the 329th, he will be amazed at the wealth of world-traveled men to be found. For example, Joseph Truskolowski was born on August 1, 1919, in Detroit, Mich. When Joe was 2 years old, his parents moved back to Poland. He attended elementary and high school in his home town of Bialystok and then he attended Lyceum College. During his first years of college he received Glider training which whetted his taste for flying. In his last year, Russia occupied Poland, and Russian was added to his curriculum. Besides Polish, Joe speaks German, English and Russian.

Joseph Truskolowski

"In December 1939, Joe went to Moscow to try and get his passport so that he could return to the United States. He encountered a great deal of trouble and, after trying for a week, he decided to return to Warsaw and contact the American Ambassador to see if he could get some help. However, he learned that he would have to sneak across the closely guarded frontier to get back to Poland. While he was doing this, he was sighted by a Russian sentry, who fired at him. Joe, however, wasn't hit and he continued to Warsaw.

"After seeing the American Ambassador in

Warsaw, Joe returned to Bialystok where he remained until November of '40. He was then notified that his passport was ready. He returned to Moscow and while final arrangements were being made, he spent time visiting Lenin's tomb, the Kremlin and other historic spots in Moscow. When final arrangements were completed, Joe journeyed by train through Siberia to Vladivolstok. He sailed from Vladivolstok on a small Japanese tramp steamer and landed at the port of Kanazowa in Japan Proper. He completely crossed Japan from Kanazowa to Tokyo by train in 12 hours.

"After spending two weeks in Tokyo, Joe sailed to the U.S. on the USS Cleveland. He landed in San Francisco on January, 2, 1941, and promptly went to New York to live with his sister who came from Poland in 1929. Joe's first job in America was that of interpreter in a New York court of law. He left this position however, for a job with the Worthing Pump Co. in New Jersey. Like almost all the young men in the U.S., Joe found his civilian life cut short when his number came up, and on April 27, 1942, he discovered himself a member of the U.S. Army. He was sent to Ft. Eustas, Va., for three months basic training and was then transferred to an anti-aircraft unit in Camp Davis, N.C. While at Camp Davis, Joe earned the rank of sergeant.

"In August 1943, Joe joined the Air Corps and came to Slippery Rock through Kessler Field with the present 'D' Squadron. Joe likes S.R. very much, having met several Polish families in New Castle who have shown him very warm and friendly attitudes. Joe's parents, together with one sister and three brothers, are still in Poland. He hasn't heard from them since July of '42, and he believes the Nazis have forced two of his brothers to work in the factories. Joe hopes that his next trip to Poland will be in a bomber. May all your wishes come true, Joe."

A very significant problem throughout the college training program was lack of time. Little could be done about this since the basic requirements of the program necessitated that a certain amount of time be spent on various phases. Despite the fact that there were two hours available nightly for study, most students could not complete all of their academic work in that time. An additional period with academic supervision was added on Sunday for those with failing grades, and some marks were brought up. Lack of standardization in testing, especially in math, caused failures in math classes due to different testing standards. This created a morale problem since failures meant loss of Open Post privileges on weekends. Several academic instructors were "teaching over the heads" of the average student. Both issues were corrected.

Academic success became more of an issue with subsequent incoming classes. From the records of these students, the educational background was getting poorer than the previous classes. Early in the program each class had a fairly high percentage of men with college work, but these dwindled until only a few had any college training. The last classes in 1943 were composed of many non-high school graduates. They were lost, often in math and physics, after the first few classes in simple fundamentals, Commander Stephens wrote. There was a lack of incentive to attain high marks, and "taking away Open Post privileges created little incentive. Academic learning seemed to follow the adage 'You can lead a horse to water but you can't make him drink.' No one could force an aviation student to learn despite all efforts to make studying highly necessary to keep in good standing. The fact that academic eliminations were not permitted was a distinct drawback. They had the attitude that they couldn't be eliminated and so had little more than ordinary incentive to study. Evaluation of their academic accomplishment will only become apparent after the graduating class has started their next phase of the flying training."

Because of the informal nature of academic instruction under college teachers, there was a great tendency to forget the military side of their training. Some cadets developed the attitude that they were not soldiers, but merely college students. The Station Historic Report states, "In the majority of cases, the aviation student had been in the army four or five weeks, just long enough to finish basic training. Upon arrival at college, where all accommodations are very superior to basic training, there seems to be a feeling that the army has been left behind and that he is back in college. It's a difficult task to make that cadet realize the seriousness of the present emergency and the long, hard months of training yet ahead of him. In three isolated cases, it was evident that the only desire of the student was to spend five months in college, enjoying a safe and comfortable existence, and then when the time came for him to commit to be a pilot, bombardier or navigator, he deliberately 'washed out.' In instances like these, officers and pilots who had returned from overseas counseled the cadets in the difficulties that lay ahead, especially in combat. The 8th were regularly shown GI movies, and taken as a unit to local theatres to war movies for an 'in-your-face' reality check." Some had a poor military bearing, as well as a lack of ability to give military commands, reports or explanations. Few of the aviation cadets could accept the answer "no" but attempted to argue and quibble about matters of military nature with their officers. Pressure of a disciplinary nature was continuously exerted to correct this deficiency. Due to the unusual amount of time in the academic classroom, the aviation students had a tendency to become lax in all military standards. The Commanding Officer and Training Officers recommended a much greater emphasis be placed on general military training.

1st Lt. Francis T. Stephens was named Commanding Officer of the 8th Detachment at Grove City College on January 7, 1944, and replaced 1st Lt. Frederick E. Green.

CHAPTER 6

Mission Accomplished - Too Soon It Ends

The general morale of the 8th Detachment since activation through January 7, 1944, was good. There were factors, however, that worked to undermine it: failure of the Commanding Officer to use the cadets' Unit Fund Money to provide entertainment (it collected and sat there); friction between Commander Green and other Officers, as well as between the permanent party and Green; and Commander Green's policy of using academic deficiencies for Closed Post weekends (many cadets had not left the barracks for several consecutive months during weekends). Green's Closed Post enforcement lead to a "What-the-hell-is-the-use?" feeling and unauthorized absences.

From March '43 to March '44, the 8th Training Detachment had 13 convictions by Summary Courts Martial; all offenses were "absence without leave" and there were no recurrences. There were 20 punishments under the 104th Article of War for the following offenses: violation of Open Post privilege, absent without leave, off post during restricted hours, arrogant remarks to physical instructor, shirking duty in class, direct disregard for military discipline and utter indifference toward habits pertaining thereto, unauthorized

extension of liberty, violation of post regulation, violation of Code of Ethics and striking an aviation student officer. No offense recurred.

Conversely, working toward building morale were the cooperation and friendly spirit extended to all aviation students by members of the community and churches, as well as by the college, including the academic instructors; the importance attached to the ultimate goal of training for each aviation student; and the belief and aspiration to live up to the high standards of military achievement maintained by the Air Corps.

The first official inspection by Army Air Forces Southeast Training Center of facilities and equipment was on April 27, 1943. On August 18, 19 and 20, an inspection was conducted by Maj. Leslie Thompson from Maxwell Field. Recommendations and deficiencies concerned the administrative section, the student organization, academic facilities, recreation, messing facilities, quarters, supply, medical facilities, college authorities and religious activities. The general rating was "very satisfactory." However, the second endorsement to the report requiring further explanation of several discrepancies in the report of inspection and the third endorsement, which was the Commanding Officer's answer, were later found missing from the files of the 8th Detachment, and no explanation can be offered for their absence.

On November 17, 1943, the 8th was visited by academic inspectors from Randolph Field, Texas. They found that the program needed certain changes and recommended such to Commander Green and the academic coordinator. These recommendations were based on personal conferences and given verbally, hence no official record can be quoted. But Academic Coordinator Dr. H.O. White later offered that classes would be held five times weekly instead of three times, and a remedial study period from 1900 to 2000 hours Monday through Friday, supervised by instructors, would be implemented for deficient students.

On January 4, 1944, two Captains from Randolph Field, one being the Assistant Director of Training, made an academic inspection. They noted further deficiencies in the academic program. A request for changes was made verbally and written requirements were submitted to the Commanding Officer for his compliance. On January 7, 1944, Commanding Officer Green was succeeded by 1st Lt. Francis T. Stephens. Numerous administrative, medical, academic and military changes were accomplished almost immediately.

The Annual General Inspection of the 8th Detachment was conducted by Maj. Paul McMurray and 1st Lt. Charles Biggs from Randolph Field on February 4, 1944. They gave an overall rating of "excellent." "The officers of the college have manifested an admirable spirit of cooperation toward the college training detachment from its beginning and have contributed to a high standard of discipline and morale," they wrote. On February 25, 1944, an informal inspection was made by Maj. W.J. Hayes and, during conferences with all members of the Officer Staff, commendation was expressed for the entire training program and facilities.

Just after midnight on January 30, 1944, the college received a telegram from an officer of the Army Air Corps saying that the contract between the college and the Army Air Corps was to be terminated. The February 1944 Grove City College Alumni News stated, "Under the new plan announced by the military authorities, the cadets now in college will finish their courses. However, no new cadets are to be sent to the cam-

Army Air Corps Training Program Is Discontinued

Cadets Now Enrolled At Grove City Will Finish Courses

Just after midnight, Sunday, January 30th, the College received a telegram from a district officer of the Army Air Corps saying that the contract between the College and the Army Air Corps was to be terminated. Under the plan announced by the military authorities the cadets now in College will finish their courses. However, no new cadets are to be sent to the campus. As a result, the program will be liquidated sometime during the month of May. While the action taken by the military author-

The success of the Air Corps program at the College was indicated by a report made by Major Pearl W. McMurray of the Inspection General's Department who inspected the Air Corps on February 4. At that time, the Grove City College detachment received a rating of "excellent" which is the highest rating attainable.

The report of the inspection contained the following paragraph:

"The officers of the college have manifested an admirable spirit of cooperation toward the college training detachment from its beginning and have contributed to a high standard of discipline and morale. The co-ordinator of the college training program is Dr. H. O. White."

The cessation of pre-flight training in many colleges may indicate that the peak of the training program in the present war has been passed. We only hope that it may indicate that the end of the war is close at hand and that before many months the College may be able to reestablish its peace-time program.

The success of the Air Corps program at the College was indicated by a report made by Major Pearl W. McMurray of the Inspection General's Department who inspected the Air Corps on February 4. At that time, the Grove City College detachment received a rating of "excellent" which is the highest rating attainable.

The report of the inspection contained the following paragraph:

"The officers of the college have manifested an admirable spirit of cooperation toward the college training detachment from its beginning and have contributed to a high standard of discipline and morale. The co-ordinator of the college training program is Dr. H. O. White."

The cessation of pre-flight training in many colleges may indicate that the peak of the training program in the present war has been passed. We only hope that it may indicate that the end of the war is close at hand and that before many months the College may be able to reestablish its peace-time program.

The Grove City College Bulletin in February 1944 told the news of the discontinuation of the CPTP.

pus. As a result, the program will be liquidated sometime during the month of May, but no later than June 30, 1944. The termination of the program will involve a reorganization of the program of the college and will, of necessity, create problems of administrative and financial character. The cessation of the pre-flight training in many colleges may indicate that the peak of the training program in the present war has been passed. We only hope that it may indicate that the end of the war is close at hand and that before many months the college may be able to reestablish its peace-time program."

The Army Air Corps' official announcement stated it was planning to end all War Training Service flight instructor training. The production rate of pilots within the system, in addition to pilots returning from combat, was adequate to handle current needs. The announcement expressed appreciation of the excellent work accomplished by the flight contractors, ground schools and CAA personnel who were engaged in the training of pilots for the Air Forces. The Chief or Commanding General of the Army Air Corps was Henry H. "Hap" Arnold. He had placed many stumbling blocks in the program's way: refusing to cooperate with the CAA and Congress in making full use of the program; imposing unrealistic training goals and quotas; and giving little or no assistance for the required training. The Corps preferred instead to train its own pilots without what it considered civilian interference. During 1943-44, the Army Air Corps trained 55,348 enlisted reservists in a variety of pilot specialties. The average cost per cadet was a modest

$628.16. By CAA statistics, these men were better prepared for military aviation training than those who had not been through the program and less likely to fail.

On March 1, 1944, the 8th College Training Detachment was in the preparatory stage of deactivation pursuant to directions received on February 7, 1944, from Army Air Corps Central Flying Training Command, Randolph Field, Texas. In accordance with this directive, classes were reduced in size and no further replacements were received by the detachment. On March 30, Hap Arnold sent a telegram titled "Surplus Air Crew Trainees." It directed that only trainees who qualified under certain categories would be permitted to continue training as aviation students. The rest would be relieved from aircrew training. "It is desired that all men to be withdrawn be thoroughly oriented with respect to the decisions reached in order that their morale may not be lowered by the unfounded rumors and ill-informed speculation. For this purpose, you will direct the commanding officer to take the following steps immediately:

a. Assemble a meeting of all the men to inform them of the facts. The following telegram should be read by an officer, and a suitable true copy will be given to each man. You will return to the Ground and Service Forces all enlisted men who have volunteered from these sources and have been found fully qualified for training as pilots, bombardiers and navigators, but who have not yet entered pre-flight school. This action is necessary as the result of a critical and immediate need for young, vigorous and well-trained men with

ABOVE: Fuzzy, center, stands with his March '44 Group 1 Class. BELOW: Fuzzy scrawls notes on the back of a March '44 picture.

Sat. 3/18/44
Did not fly this P.M. due to a strong wind.
Had just told Bodenman to write South pattern
50 times for not knowing pattern in 6th lesson
Also went 250 ft. too high in pattern.

leadership qualifications to meet the urgent need of the Ground and Service Forces. It is essential that every one of these soldiers be made available for pending operations in view of accumulated shortages that have developed since last July in Selective Service. It is with profound regret that I consent to drop from the team these spirited young men who have aspired to join our combat crews who are gaining for us superiority in the air in every theater of warfare. It is, however, the very success of the teams now in combat that makes this shift of fighting power wise and proper. We must present a balanced front to our enemies. The team has succeeded better than we dared hope for when our quotas were set and it now permits a reduction in our training rate. I am sure that these men will understand that in a program of such magnitude there will be times when the number of men who qualify will exceed the quota for that period. While it is my duty to regard this matter in a practical light, it is my desire that you hand each of these men a copy of this message explaining the reasons for his being obliged to forego this training. Will you also convey my personal appreciation and thanks for his interest and wish him good luck and good hunting in the branch to which he returns. I am confident that these fine American soldiers who want to do the greatest possible damage to the enemy will prefer the opportunity for an earlier engagement to the alternative of waiting for training at some later date.

b. The following entry will be made in each man's service record: 'Accepted for aircrew training, relieved without prejudice for the convenience of the government.'"

1st Lt. Francis Stephens, Commanding Officer, "immediately formed the 23 men who were affected by this directive … into a group and carried out the instructions, and answered all pertinent questions insofar as possible. … Their service record would also be altered to say, 'Accepted for aircrew training, relieved without prejudice for the convenience of the government.'"

The next few weeks, Stephens continues, "were a series of orders and counter-orders (very chaotic) that readied the permanent party (the college) and officers for the actual closing down process. Of the 111 CPTP students still at Grove City, the lucky ones moved on to pilot training, but 62 aviation students were shuttled (for the convenience of the government) into other fields of duty in the Army Air Forces or other arms and services . Underneath there is another picture, not as tangible but still existing none the less. It is the morale factor: the effect of these Army Air Force measures on the aviation students in training here at the time. Newspaper articles and radio commentators had pointed the way in announcing a switch of some 36,000 Army Air Force personnel eligible for aircrew training to other branches of service. AAF officials explained this as a necessary step to speedier victory. 'Personnel losses,' so Headquarters stated, 'were decidedly less than anticipated'; thus the turnover of AAF trainees to former Arms and Services. First word of this change had a rather demoralizing effect on the students concerned. When the various groups were brought together and messages explaining this action by Headquarters read to them, they were sick at heart. There was no denying the fact.

However, these men are to be commended on the way they did camouflage their disappointment and accept their new status in the Army. That they fell in line with the orders from their superiors as readily as they did speaks well for the type of men chosen for flight training and also for the effect that preliminary training had on their behavior."

Right in the middle of the disbandment, on April 14, Stephens received General Order #14, calling for "Organization of Certain Army Air Force Base Units." The 8th College Training Detachment was to be called the 2581st AAF Base Unit and assume its re-designation on May 1, 1944. Stephens, with humor, commented, "a copy of the Order was posted and interested agencies of the government were notified. As might be expected, the official mail being received is addressed to the 8th Detachment. Coming at a time when disbandment procedure is in progress, it's rather ironic." It was like a basketball number being retired, but never hung in the rafters. After a while, the player, without identity, and his story are forgotten.

Signs of spring were apparent at the airport. Early flowering bulbs and bushes could be seen at the adjoining McCoy farm. And late in the day, peepers could be heard from the swamp areas and the creek. As enrollment dropped, there was a slight curtailment in shop and instruction personnel. Office help and line boys stayed the same. From 40 students at peak time, there were 31 aviation students now, but getting more instruction time from the five instructors. The instruction program remained the same in policy and coverage. Chief Pilot Tyndall was now their only superior. For this final class of instruction, six Piper J-3s were sufficient for flying use.

Aviation Student Flight Training for the 8th Detachment was consummated on the evening of April 27, 1944. After the last Cub landed, the line boys put the planes to bed in the hangar and slowly closed the massive door.

The next day, the final shipment out of those remaining students was accomplished, and the disbandment of the administrative department began. First a detailed inventory was conducted, and then a disbursement of correspondence, bank accounts, all property and equipment was made to various sites around the country. This took several weeks of intense work. On May 1, 1944, the Grove City Airport and Wilson Aviation were released from further government contractor's agreements and the management of the airport began offering its services to private interests. On May 4, 1944, the 329th Detachment from Slippery Rock completed flight training at the airport. The final report from Grove City Airport was submitted to Military Headquarters on May 6, 1944. Though extremely busy with details of closing, once the airport was opened for civilian use, Francis T. Stephens signed up personally for flying lessons. In record time, he learned the fundamentals from either Birch or Fuzzy or both. On May 22, near the end of his Grove City tour, he took off alone in a Piper Cub and soared above the town. The officer-turned-student is the second person listed on the Boards with his May 22, 1944, solo date.

On May 31, 1944, Commander Stephens sat at his desk with hands on a manual typewriter. And, as his last act before the impending transfer to Lubbock Air Force Base, Texas, he issued the letter at right and below.

HEADQUARTERS
2581ST AAF BASE UNIT
(COLLEGE TRAINING AIRCREW)
GROVE CITY COLLEGE

31 May 1944

Discontinuance of 2581st AAF Base Unit (College Training Aircrew)

Pursuant to authority contained in General Order 26, Headquarters, Army Air Force Training Command, Fort Worth, Texas, dated 30 May 1944, the 2581st AAF Base Unit (College Training Aircrew), Grove City College, Grove City, Penna, is discontinued effective this date.

FRANCIS T. STEPHENS
1st Lieut., Air Corps
Commanding

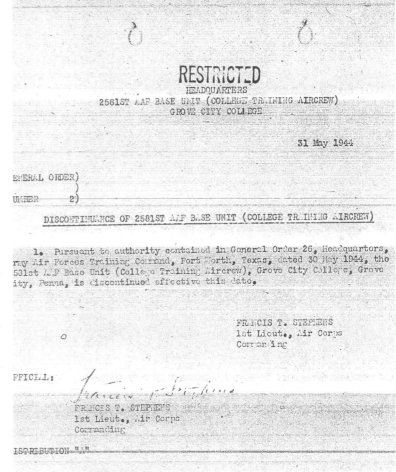

With this class, 486 students of the 8th Detachment were given flight instruction with almost 5,000 hours. The average number of instruction hours given by flight instructors was 947, an average of 66.5 hours per month. Gardner Birch flew 910 hours in 12 months.

Stephens reported, "cooperation and efficiency of the administrative and instructor staff of the Grove City Airport left nothing to be desired. At no time was there any difficulty experienced with the flying part of the aviation program. According to our best knowledge, the flight instruction accomplished the mission of the College Training Program."

The cadets were taught to fly for their country's safety and to fly proud.

Many of these historic facts were discovered in December 2005, a year into this project, in a document titled, "Station Historical Report of the Eighth College Training Detachment (Aircrew), Grove City College, Grove City, PA from 1 March 1943 to 1 March 1944." It also included a 60-day report covering the disbandment of the detachment. I was searching the Internet and found a site new to me called the Air Force Historical Studies Office, located in Washington, D.C., at the Anacostia Naval Annex and part of the Air Force History and Museums Program, headquartered at the Pentagon. Prior queries to any government agency had come up empty. I e-mailed this office, and a response came back that a report existed on the Grove City Detachment and that it mentioned my dad. For a small fee, the Air Force Historical Research Agency at Maxwell Air Force Base copied the reel of microfilm of more than 200 pages. Voila! I finally had government validation of a government program that no other government agency or department would or could acknowledge up to this time.

The men and women involved with the 8th Detachment and the Grove City Airport during the Civilian Pilot Training Program are well into their 70s, if not older, now. I believe all of the instructors and military leaders are deceased, but I have spoken to some of their relatives. Because the cadets were not local, I have not talked to anyone who trained in the program at the college. I have spoken to a few men who trained under the CPTP elsewhere. I can only hope that this writing will introduce me to someone from the 8th Detachment. Here is more on some men and women who are only mentioned in Part I.

Judd Youkers, Gardner and Fuzzy's initial instructor, likewise served in the CPTP/WTS. Though relatively young, his vast experience and conservative nature landed him the position of Chief CPTP Pilot at Bernard Airport. Hinkle Flying Service did the flight instruction at Bernard for Youngstown (Ohio) College. After the program disbanded that spring, Judd joined Youngstown Airways at Youngstown Municipal Airport. On Armistice Day, November 1944, Winston Churchill and Charles de Gaulle led a military parade up the Champs Elysees to the Tomb of the Unknown Soldier at the Arc de Triomphe. Youkers, considered one of the most skilled pilots in the area, was flying home from a chartered hunting trip late in the afternoon. There was a low ceiling with fog and icing in the clouds. Twenty miles from home, Youkers got off course and was flying low, possibly blind in the clouds. Nearby residents saw the plane drop two parachute flares as Youkers sought a field for an emergency landing. At 6:12 p.m. they heard a crash.

His five-passenger Stinson monoplane had hit the top of a tree. Three bodies were thrown clear of the wreckage. A half-dozen rabbits, some ruffed grouse, pheasants and hunting gear were scattered near the crumpled fuselage. At age 35, Judd Youkers was killed instantly. The veteran commercial pilot and instructor left a wife and three children.

Instructor Brenton Holter started a bus company in Grove City, both school buses and charter service. Wendall Miles worked for him for many years driving a school bus. "Brenton was a good boss, generous—he'd give you the shirt off his back. He used to have safety meetings and gave orders to his drivers like 'Never back up the bus. If you get to the intersection and can't make a turn, make the cars back up, not you.' Next day, Brenton had to fill in for a driver, and one of the other employees saw him backing up his bus to make a turn. He later sold the business to his daughter and died around 1992."

Seymour Heinberg went on to Texas with the Air Corps. He then returned to his wife, Bea, in New York City and continued his Certified Public Accounting practice. They had two children and he lived a long, full life until 2003.

Ray Flanagan returned to Vermont in the spring of '44 and taught flying at a local airport. In January 1945, he returned to the Army and was stationed at Fort Devons, Mass. It was there he found out he was very sick. He died in May of 1945.

Instructor Ray Flanagan

John Subject left the Detachment, yet wanted to become a pilot. But his wife would not allow it because she wanted security and regular wages. So he went back to Olean, N.Y., to become a printer for the Olean Herald Tribune, then the Buffalo Currier Express. He was a father of three. At his death, he had retired to Florida.

Lawyers were always a major part of John Henderson's life. John's first passenger as a pilot was Milford "Miff" McBride, who was still practicing law in Grove City in 2007. After his instructor days, John went to law school and became a judge in Lawrence County, Pa., for 29 years. He flew out of Fin's New Castle Airport through the late 1950s. His son, David, also an attorney, married Miff and Madeleine Coulter McBride's daughter, Brenda. Brenda is an attorney with her dad's firm of McBride and McBride. The firm began more than 85 years ago and is a legend in Grove City. They searched and prepared many of the deeds in the chain of title for both the old Grove City Airport and Fin's Sharon Airport.

Jeanne Carruthers got a bachelor of science degree in commerce from Grove City College, and married Norman Davidson, a mechanical engineering student. She worked as a secretary at Leo Stevenson's machine shop on Park Street from 1946-49. She then followed her husband while he worked for General Electric, once known as Pennsylvania Electric. She currently winters in Florida and summers near State College, Pa.

Margaret Fithian was Jeanne's sorority sister in Gamma Chi at Grove City. While at college, she met and married Gerald Bovard. He became a business professor at the University of Texas in El Paso, then went back to Grove City College in

1976 to teach business. Margaret took additional classes but was primarily a stay-at-home mom. The Bovards live with their daughter and family near West Chester, Pa.

The written update to Grove City College is from the best possible source. Dick Jewell, a 1967 graduate of Grove City College, had as his instructors some of the same teachers the cadets did in the '40s. Now Dr. Jewell, a Pittsburgh lawyer and business leader, is the President of Grove City College, a post he began in 2003 and loves. He writes:

"In the post-World War II era, both the college and the Borough of Grove City saw continued growth. The college was led by Dr. Weir Ketler, a 1908 graduate of Grove City, until 1956, then in the last 10 years of his 40-year presidential service at Grove City. Between 1950 and 1960, enrollment grew from 1,278 to about 1,500, further growing to 2,090 in 1970, 2,253 in 1980, with a slight decline to 2,138 in 1990 until an all time record 2,489 in the fall of 2006. The 40-year Ketler era took the college from its pioneer foundation days under founder Dr. Isaac C. Ketler (Weir's father) to its growing years of academic strength and financial security.

"Under the leadership of Dr. J. Stanley Harker, a '25 graduate and President from 1956-1971) major new buildings such as Hoyt Hall of Engineering and Calderwood Hall, plus additional residence halls for women, such as Helen Harker Hall, were constructed. Also, due to a number of retirements in the early Harker years, many new faculty were hired.

"The 20-year administration of Dr. Charles S. MacKenzie also saw continued faculty renewal, the construction of the magnificent J. Howard Pew Fine Arts Center, the new Weir C. Ketler Technological Learning Center and a large expansion to the college's Physical Learning Center. Under Dr. MacKenzie, the college's Christian mission was strengthened and continued to reaffirm the school's virtues of faith and freedom. Also under Dr. MacKenzie, the college sued the United States federal government in a dispute that went all the way to the United States Supreme Court. At issue was the Fed's insistence that the college subscribe to and be subject to a new federal regulation (Title IX). The college asserted that the federal government had no jurisdiction because the school took no direct federal money. As a result of the case, the college received, in the court's opinion, a roadmap to be able to follow and to therefore definitively avoid Title IX and, in fact, certain other federal requirements and mandates. The case pitted David (Grove City College) versus Goliath (the federal government) and was viewed favorably by many as an example of an institution with strong principles standing up for what it believes.

"The years of President Jerry H. Combee saw focused curricular revisions as well as the emergence of the college at the top tier of many national rankings for both academics and affordability. The administrations of Dr. John H. Moore (1996-2003) and Dr. Dick Jewell '67 saw the beginning and completion of a $68 million dollar capital campaign that supported the building of a new Hall of Arts and Letters, a new Student Union, a dramatic addition to the Pew Fine Arts Center, an addition in 2008-09 to the Carnegie Alumni

Center on lower campus, plus $25 million in student scholarship assistance.

"In addition, under the Board of Trustees' leadership and in conjunction with the administration of Dr. Jewell, a new first-ever five-year strategic plan was prepared and implemented with the following vision statement: 'To be one of America's premier liberal arts, science and engineering colleges, where scholarship combines with Christian principles.'

"From its founding in 1876 until the beginning of WWII, the college was a strong local school. From the end of WWII until the mid 1980s, it was a noted and strong multi-state/regional campus. And from 1985 or so through today, it is a school that draws outstanding students from across the nation and around the world. The dream of its founder, Dr. Isaac Ketler, positioned well those who succeeded him in presidential leadership. Supported by involved college Trustees, Grove City College is now one of our nation's leading (and so recognized) institutions of higher education.

"Likewise, the Borough of Grove City has grown apace with the college since the end of WWII. Fueled by a strong agra/dairy business base, on land from which much coal was extracted, along with a heavy industrial base, as evidenced by the Cooper-Bessemer plant, the local economy had strong results. While the Cooper-Bessemer plant closed in 1999, two different but significant economic drivers came on the scene. First, General Electric built a large plant to make railroad locomotive motors in town in 1984. And in 1994, one of the largest outlet malls in the country, now known as Prime Outlets Grove City, opened five miles out of downtown at the Grove City exit of Interstate 79. Both of these ventures have added to the business mix of the area. In addition, numerous high-tech businesses have opened and prospered in the community. Also, in the early 1980s, a new community hospital, now named Grove City Medical Center, was formed out of the merger of two long-existing hospitals. Today that medical center provides hundreds of jobs and is a regional focal point for health care.

"The 1980s and '90s saw a number of long-time downtown businesses cease operation. To revitalize the downtown using federal, state and donated private capital (of which Grove City College was the lead private-sector donor), a $3 million-plus refurbishing is planned for completion in the fall of 2007. As part of that change, the college purchased the Grove City Diner property, which it will use for additional parking. The goal is to reinvigorate and renew the downtown area into a vibrant commercial sector once again."

- *Jane Gardner Birch*
- *Richard G. Jewell*

PART II:

THE SOLO BOARDS

BOARD 1

"The end of the Civilian Pilot Training Program/War Service Training Program took its toll financially and in more personal terms on the 5,000 military trainees in varying stages of training, enlisted reserve flight instructors and the fixed based operators who conducted flight training. The end of the program meant frustration and, in some cases, a loss of livelihood for these people," Dominick Pisano explains.

As a result of the program's abrupt end, neither the CAA nor the AAF had planned for assimilating the trainees and instructors into the workforce. The perceived arbitrariness of the AFF's decision made many men feel that they had been badly used. It denied any responsibility other than to make opportunities available to qualified, not all, men. An article in the local newspaper at that time tells the story:

The 21 pilots in the ready room of the Grove City Airport predicted they would be "the forgotten men" of the Army Air Force by May 15, 1944. Scores like them in the Pittsburgh area and 5,000 of them in the nation foresee the same destiny. These birdmen sincerely believe they have made one of the greatest contributions to a well-trained, quickly built air force. Now they foresee their thousands of flying hours about to be "poured down the drain," while the armed forces still are drafting men and women and training them from the ground up to do jobs these "forgotten men" believe they are fitted to do now.

Out at the airport, the War Training Service has just completed training its 1,847th pilot for the Army. R.B. Tyndall, Grove City's Chief Pilot, explains, "That leaves us pilots, many of us having 800 to 1,600 hours flying time, either to enter the service anywhere in the Army except the flying department of the Air Force or to be drafted. We were turned down when we tried to enlist in the Ferry Command or Air Transport Service. Now we have the choice of going into active service or asking for a discharge in which case we will be drafted.

"Our claim is that the government today is taking thousands of women (WASPs) who have 35 hours of flying time and training them to ferry planes. Here we're already seasoned pilots and we stand a good chance of being sent to cooks' or bakers' school. All these instructors believe there are plenty of jobs they can do in the Air Force. All over the nation, the thousands of us War Training Service Instructors are trying to rouse public opinion so that a few regulations can be changed so our experience will not go down the drain while millions of dollars are being spent to train others to learn to do what we already can do," Tyndall concluded.

Nationally, the fixed base operators were mad as hornets and grouped under umbrella organizations for an extension of the CPTP bill. They were loath to relinquish a federally subsidized program that put money into their coffers and that had caused flight training and small airport operations to prosper as never before. But it was for naught.

It wasn't the habit in Western Pennsylvania to sit and sulk or cry over spilled milk. The lucrative contract had evaporated as of May 1, 1944, and so the airport would have to reinvent itself. Fin Wilson put Gardner Birch in charge of the Grove City Airport, and Fuzzy DeArment was his sidekick. They would have to hustle new ways of generating income, in addition to dealing with the major difficulty of gasoline rationing. For the time that the CPTP was using the airport under government contract, gas for the planes was not a problem. Now in civilian mode, it was. Lessons could only be given on days that gasoline was delivered. Working within this limitation, income would have to come from civilian instruction, aviation services and fees, and from training returning soldiers to fly using the GI Bill of Rights.

America has traditionally compensated its veterans for their services. In 1636, the Pilgrims declared, "If any person shall be sent forth as a soldier and shall return maimed, he shall be maintained competently by the Colony during his life." Early in the Revolutionary War, the Continental Congress created the first veterans' benefit package, which included lifelong pensions for both disabled veterans and dependents of soldiers killed in battle. Educational benefits date back to the beginning of the 20th century. Congress recognized that military service prevented young peo-

ple from receiving training for employment or a vocation and passed the Rehabilitation Act of 1919, giving disabled WWI vets a monthly education assistance allowance. This was in addition to any end-of-service pay. The Stars and Stripes publication of August 10, 1944, reported, "Added to whatever we can save from our monthly pay will be the 'mustering out' pay of $300 (a final payment for military service, paid in three monthly installments), beginning the day some officer hands us our discharge papers and says, 'Soldier, you're now a civilian.'"

As the U.S. entered WWII, there were very mixed feelings in Congress and at colleges and universities about how post-war benefits should be handled. But dire economic predictions for the post-war years created great pressure to pass offsetting legislation. Many saw America faced with a loss of millions of jobs, creating unprecedented unemployment and another possible widespread depression. Memories were fresh from 1929. The National Resources Planning Board in June of '43 recommended a series of programs for education and training. But it was the American Legion that is credited with designing the main features of the GI Bill and pushing it through Congress on June 13, 1944. President Roosevelt signed it into law on June 22, even before the war ended.

The first GI Bill provided six benefits: education and training; loan guaranty for a home, farm, or business; unemployment pay of $20 per week for up to 52 weeks; job-search assistance; top priority for building materials for VA hospitals; and military review of dishonorable discharges.

To be eligible for GI Bill education benefits, a WWII veteran had to serve 90 days or more after

September 16, 1940, and have other than a dishonorable discharge. Veterans of the war were entitled to one year of full-time training plus a period equal to their time in service, up to a maximum of 48 months. VA paid the educational institutions up to a maximum of $500 per year for tuition, books, fees and other training costs. VA also paid the single veteran a subsistence allowance of up to $50 a month. The returning vet who wanted to become a commercial pilot had his flight lessons covered by the GI Bill.

Facts were that one out of three GIs had less than an eighth-grade education, one in six had less than a fourth-grade education and only 40 percent had completed high school. Yet out of the 15,440,000 veteran population, some 7.8 million received further training, including: 2,230,000 in college; 3,480,000 in other schools; 1,400,000 in on-the-job training; and 690,000 in farm training.

The total cost of the WWII education program was $14.5 billion. Millions who would have flooded the labor market instead opted for education, which reduced joblessness during the demobilization period. Economists have estimated that the average veteran paid two to eight times in income taxes what he or she received in educational benefits. When that vet did enter the labor market, most were better prepared to contribute to the support of their families and society because of that education. The National Education Associa-tion president said in 1995 that "(t)he GI Bill turned out to be one of the wisest investments the United States had ever made. Funding education by choice was proven to be more effective than funding education by compulsion." And the bill helped funnel dollars into the airport economy, too.

In the spring and early summer of '44, the war was going strong, especially in Europe. American military troops were making progress against the Germans. Americans at home were giving their all for the war. Many small, non-essential businesses in Grove City, like the airport, were trying to prosper and be patriotic while adapting to war circumstances. Rationing, a shortage of workers and other necessities, restrictions and tight security were all commonplace now. President Roosevelt told members of Congress, "The overwhelming majority of our people have met the demands of this war with magnificent courage and understanding. They have accepted inconveniences; they have accepted hardships; they have accepted tragic sacrifices. And they are ready and eager to make whatever further contributions are needed to win the war as quickly as possible." From one-man businesses to the town's war-essential behemoth and leader Cooper-Bessemer, locals rallied to the cause.

But who was Cooper-Bessemer? The 1895 discovery of oil underground in Titusville, Pa., required engines to drive drills and pump oil, but steam engines proved costly to operate. In 1898, Dr. Edwin Fithian and John Carruthers formed the forerunner to the Bessemer Gas Engine Company and produced kits to convert steam engines into the new internal combustion engines. Fueled with oil-field natural gas that had previously been escaping from the casing heads, gasoline was transformed from a waste product into a treasured commodity. These engines made possible the early development of the petroleum products that fueled industrial development beginning at the turn of the 20th century.

The company, which had located in the small town of Grove City, population 400, next took a natural step into gas engine manufacturing. Bessemer enlarged its line steadily. It continued to anticipate and answer the needs of oil producers. But it diversified, too, into oil engines for industrial power, irrigation, cotton ginning and mining. WWI created a surge for its huge natural gas engines, and then the diesel engine.

Bessemer Gas Engine Company's national reputation was backed by the slogan, "You buy the BEST when you buy the BESSEMER." The company built its products heavier and stronger than necessary to prevent costly repair shutdowns. It grew until it was in a competitive field dominated by C. & G. Cooper & Co. of Mt. Vernon, Ohio, and Grove City was a one-industry town.

United States energy consumption was growing rapidly in 1928. Manufacturing was enjoying boom conditions here and abroad. C. & G. Cooper was the recognized leader in pipeline compression engines. Cooper needed additional production facilities. Bessemer was hard-pressed for new capital to continue diesel development. The companies were drawing closer to designing parallel product lines. Both could gain efficiency by combining research, engineering and sales.

By 1929, Cooper had 33 buildings and 765 employees. Bessemer had 29 buildings, including one of the world's largest industrial-plant foundries (500,000 square feet and still standing), and 1,180 employees. Earnings were almost identical. After negotiating through the winter, the companies agreed on merger terms. On April 4, 1929, The Cooper-Bessemer Corporation, the largest builder of gas engines and compressors in America, came into being and was soon listed on the American Stock Exchange. Beatty B. "B.B." Williams, president of Cooper since 1920, became president and general manager. Corporate offices remained in Mt. Vernon. The ease of transition at executive levels was enhanced greatly by the personality of B.B. Williams. The supervisory personnel of the two plants blended seamlessly into a single organization. But in the shops, change was nearly imperceptible. With strong tradition ingrained, most workers thought of themselves as either "Cooper" or "Bessemer."

B.B. was a hands-on, people-orientated CEO who stressed interaction with all his workers. He was aware that an "aloofness" could develop between the offices and the shop. To remedy this, he set up conferences so shop employees could voice their views and initiated a night school so any employee could enroll in production and management classes. But heavy machinery manufacturing is highly cyclical, necessitating frequent layoffs. When the Depression hit in the fall of 1929, Williams suffered with the decisions that had to be made. On a cold December afternoon, he was walking across the square in Mt. Vernon and stopped to chat with a worker who had been recently laid off. The man had his young son with him, who obviously did not recognize the company president. Williams asked the child if he was looking forward to the holidays. "No," the child replied. "B.B. killed Santa Claus." The remark left its scar, but showed the strength of character left under the skin to go forward in very trying times. Before the October 23, 1929, crash, business had been so strong in natural gas engines, compres-

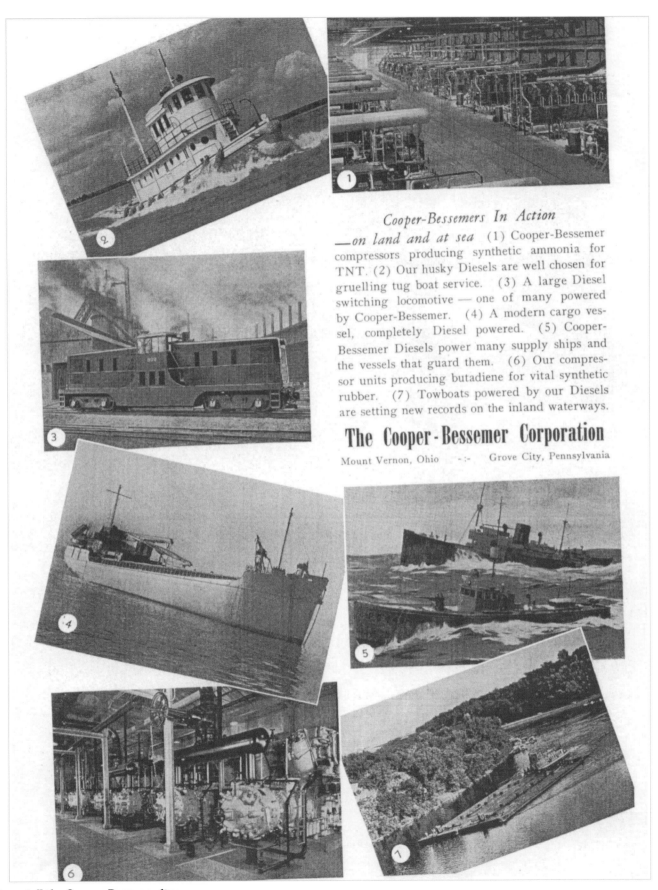

Cooper-Bessemers In Action

—on land and at sea (1) Cooper-Bessemer compressors producing synthetic ammonia for TNT. (2) Our husky Diesels are well chosen for gruelling tug boat service. (3) A large Diesel switching locomotive — one of many powered by Cooper-Bessemer. (4) A modern cargo vessel, completely Diesel powered. (5) Cooper-Bessemer Diesels power many supply ships and the vessels that guard them. (6) Our compressor units producing butadiene for vital synthetic rubber. (7) Towboats powered by our Diesels are setting new records on the inland waterways.

The Cooper-Bessemer Corporation

Mount Vernon, Ohio   -:-   Grove City, Pennsylvania

Pictures tell the Cooper-Bessemer Story.

sors and Grove City's diesel marine engines that the backlog of orders carried them forward for a year. But as Wall Street came tumbling down, Cooper-Bessemer common stock plunged from $60 to $1 a share. Annual sales in 1931 dropped 90 percent, and half of that was in the repair parts sector, forcing temporary shutdowns in parts of the plants. Although still operating at a loss, Cooper-Bessemer celebrated its 100 anniversary in 1933, announcing that it was preparing for the next 100 years. The Grove City Reporter-Herald quoted B.B. Williams as saying, "While business continues at a low ebb, we are doing many things in all departments which will help us hold our own. At present, through the operation of Share the Work, we have over 400 on our payroll."

Two accomplishments were instrumental in reestablishing the company's footing in the dismal 1930s: the diesel locomotive engine and the turbocharged diesel engine. There was a downward economic dip again in 1938, but then two steps forward. With the country's united response to the attack on Pearl Harbor, Cooper-Bessemer, like many American companies, was transformed into an official defense industry plant. The shift from civilian to military production was unprecedented. Sales skyrocketed. Military production (only 2 percent of the national output in 1939) jumped to 40 percent in 1941. America's patriotic fervor to the war is reflected in this poem by John Blair, a Cooper-Bessemer Grove City employee:

> *Our hats are off to the foundry men;*
> *Their efforts have won us the Maritime "M."*
> *Let's boost production without any yaps*
> *By hustling up with never a stop.*
> *We'll give them the bottom, while we take the top.*

COOPER-BESSEMER MEN FIRE NAVY GUNS
George Monroe and John Blair of Grove City Plant test their skill during Navy Inspection Tour. See Article on page 6.

Cooper-Bessemer workers join the Navy effort. George Monroe, left, was a longtime airport pilot.

The Maritime "M" award was presented to Cooper-Bessemer by Rear Adm. Howard Vickery at a December 18, 1942, ceremony in the Grove City plant. Workers were recognized for outstanding achievement in producing diesel engines, steam cylinder castings and other vital engine parts for cargo vessels, as well as for Liberty Ships of the U.S. fleets.

Administrative changes were altered unexpectedly amidst the company's changeover to war production. Charles Jahnke was elected president in 1940, with B.B. Williams moving to chairman of the board, succeeding Dr. Fithian, who retired. A year later, President Jahnke died suddenly of a heart attack, and Williams returned to the presidency. Enter Gordon Lefebvre, an experienced industrial executive, brought from General Motors and made vice president and general manager. Gordon would soon make his mark at Cooper-Bessemer and the airport.

Gordon Lefebvre was named vice president and general manager of Cooper-Bessemer in 1941.

The change to war manufacturing was so sudden that it posed money problems. To finance production for a $25 million contract with the Navy, Cooper-Bessemer had to work out a plan with the Pentagon to provide advance funding. Without it, payroll could not be met. Not unique to Cooper-Bessemer, such problems were common to many companies. The U.S. government financed five-sixths of the new plant construction in wartime. Win at all costs.

Patriotism dominated American thought. More than 12.4 million men and women entered the armed forces through enlistments and a draft system. Workers at Cooper-Bessemer in key production jobs hesitated to accept deferments, despite Washington's "the war will be won on the production line as well as the battle line." More than 1,200 young men, many of whom could have received an exemption, left Cooper-Bessemer for military service. Twenty-four Grove City enlistees lost their lives because of the war. Nine were missing in action, but were liberated by the Allied Armies. Women joined the work force, operating

Cooper-Bessemer CEO Gordon Lefebvre was featured on the cover the company newsletter in May of 1943.

machines and carrying out jobs previously reserved for men, as employment swelled to 4,337 on shifts that permitted round-the-clock operations. The large-scale female employment was new, startling some men. A news writer noted, "It is amazing how quickly they have adapted themselves to an entirely new line of work and how well they are doing the job." Women were blazing trails at Cooper-Bessemer and they would soon start making headlines at the airport as well.

On April 26, 1943, Gordon Lefebvre was elected president and general manager. He was high-energy and hands-on, devoting much time to improving relationships between management and labor. According to the 1943 Cooper-Bessemer News, "If you have never had the

Honor Roll of Cooper-Bessemer Now 1257

LOST IN THE SERVICE TWENTY-EIGHT

Even though one phase of this war has ended in glorious victory, the call for men from our shops continues unabated. Since our last publication fourteen more lads have gone to prepare themselves for action in the Pacific theatre of action.

Five more C-B engine-builders have lost their lives or been reported as missing in action. We have talked with most of our boys who were prisoners of war but who have been home recently on furlough. All are coming along very well.

Here's a list of those who have resigned their jobs in the past month to enter the military service:

FROM GROVE CITY PLANT

Broderick Doyle, Jr.	H. E. Hancox	R. A. Turner
R. D. Fleming, Jr.	E. L. Horkey	Wayne Walter
Joseph R. Gray	E. E. Meier, Jr.	H. R. Whitesall
	J. W. Nulph	

FROM MT. VERNON PLANT

Leland Blacksten	John Bumpus	Monte D. Keever
	Wilbur Pritchard	

(Totals to date — From Grove City 890 and from Mount Vernon 367)

CASUALTIES REPORTED TO DATE

FROM GROVE CITY PLANT:

J. R. Huff — *Killed in action*
Anthony F. Schepp — *Killed in action*
R. E. Spalding, Jr. — *Killed in action*
Anthony John — *Killed in action*
Howard S. Wilson — *Killed in action*
Gail Barber — *Killed in action*
Jay W. Palmer — *Killed in action*
Richard E. Craft — *Killed in action*
John M. McCall — *Killed in action*
Jack Mayes — *Killed in action*
Howard Cook — *Killed in action*
John S. Robinson — *Killed in action*
James E. Bestwick — *Killed in action*
Archie Ferguson — *Killed in action*
Paul Zupen — *Killed in action*

FROM GROVE CITY PLANT:

William H. Monks — *Killed in action*
John C. McCoy — *Killed in action*
Andrew Kravchuk — *Killed*
Lester Lowry — *Killed*
Walter F. Graham — *Died of wounds*
John D. Wilkins — *Died of wounds*
Lyle Cookson — *Died of wounds*
Wayne McClelland — *Missing in action*
Oliver B. Elder — *Missing in action*
Fred Nightwine — *Missing in action*
Glenn H. Rainey — *Missing in action*
*Harrison Jenkins — *Prisoner of War*
*Charles L. Keck — *Prisoner of War*
*Jos. F. Todarello — *Prisoner of War*
*Ralph E. Brown — *Prisoner of War*

(*)*Have been liberated by Allied Armies*

FROM GROVE CITY PLANT:

*Clifford Buckley — *Prisoner of War*
*Stanley Rowland — *Prisoner of War*
*Walter G. McFadden — *Prisoner of War*
*Clifford L. Allen — *Prisoner of War*
*Wm. M. Breese — *Prisoner of War*
Carman A. Patrick — *Lost at Sea*
George Rowe — *Drowned at Sea*

FROM MOUNT VERNON PLANT:

Julius M. Keck — *Killed in action*
John K. Shoemaker — *Killed in action*
Fred W. Gibson — *Died in Service*
Virgil Rose, Jr. — *Missing in action*
Frederick Miller — *Died in camp*

FROM GREGGTON, TEXAS:

K. N. Nicholson — *Missing in action*

Cooper-Bessemer recognized its World War II employees with an honor roll.

opportunity of meeting 'the boss,' don't expect to spot him about the plant attired in a Sunday suit, as on the cover. However, if you see a tall six-footer hustling from department to department, in shirt sleeves and vest, that's the man—your President."

Gordon led a hectic life. Time management was vital to strong production. And yet he had to commute the 160 miles between Mt. Vernon, Ohio, and Grove City. In addition, he was a member of the Joint War Production Committee of the Economic Defense Board, coordinating the production of war materials in the U.S. with Canada. Trips to Washington and New York and other major cities were common. "Railroad and commercial airline restrictions, as well as the current 35-mile automobile victory speed" were major problems. So a few months after taking over, in the summer of 1943, Gordon made an executive decision. Cooper-Bessemer purchased its own airplane, a new Model 45 Fairchild Low Wing Airliner, powered by a 350-horsepower Wright Model E-2 engine. With a cruising speed of 150 to 160 miles per hour and a

40-foot wing spread, and equipped with modern controls and instruments, it held five passengers. Airplanes and flying would now become part of Lefebvre's everyday life.

The chief pilot was Emmerson Bennett, a highly skilled pilot with 14 years experience. Suitable hangar and landing facilities were in place at Port Kenyon in Gambier, Ohio, and at both the Grove City and New Castle airports. Technically, these Pennsylvania airports were under military contracts that restricted civilian use. But Gordon was a master politician. He had contracts with the Navy, Cooper-Bessemer's products were used by all branches of the military, and Lefebvre was on an elite national war committee. Influence and power prevailed, and Fin received extra income.

In 1943, Cooper-Bessemer's net sales jumped to $43 million, more than tripling the all-time record of 1941. Toward the end of '43, these words from Lefebvre appeared in the Cooper-Bessemer News, "All of you fellows from Grove City and Mt. Vernon who went into the service have never been far from my thoughts. As we approach the

Cooper-Bessemer's Model 45 Fairchild is surrounded by lowly Piper Cubs. The airport shop is to the right and the McCoy barn is behind the rudder.

ABOVE: Chief pilot Emmerson Bennett stands with Cooper-Bessemer's Fairchild. BELOW: The Cooper-Bessemer News World War II Christmas Issue tried to lift up families at home.

Christmas Season, I wish it were physically possible to extend my hand and personally wish each and every one of you a Merry Christmas.

"Perhaps, too, we could chat about post-war plans—because most of you boys would like to know how we will put to use the Victory you fellows are winning for us. Naturally, the final decision regarding many of our plans depends upon the answers to some mighty important questions. For example: What about taxes? What will our government do with the plants constructed and placed in operation for war work? How can we finance our reconversion to peacetime production? How soon after cancellation of war contracts will we be paid for that portion of work completed?

"I'm quite confident that—given a political and economic environment which is favorable to the expansion of free enterprise, you can be sure that just as we are giving you what you need to win the war, we will be able to give you what you'll need to enjoy the victory. So may God bless you and a Merry Christmas to each of you."

Lefebvre led Cooper-Bessemer in the direction of product innovation and new marketing of light metals, aviation gasoline, synthetic rubber and high explosives, in addition to its core products. As a result of sizable growth and increased reputation, a more mature, powerful Cooper-Bessemer was listed on the New York Stock Exchange in 1944.

The beginning of the end to the war would occur on D-Day: June 6, 1944. Western Allies (Americans, British and Canadians) invaded German-held Normandy. This was a defining turning point, though a lot of rough fighting lay ahead in the next 14 months. Out at the airport, transition to civilian income was the focus. New ideas and new students were needed. One of the favorite recruiting places for Birch and Fuzzy was the Grove City Diner. The Diner (in business until 2005) was built in 1938, directly across from Grove City College. It was a favorite hangout for all the locals, but especially for the college gang who smoked, since this was a "no-no" on campus! Students ran across the street at breaks for a drag on a Camel or Lucky Strike. Many were solicited to take flying lessons. A long-standing tradition in the aviation industry was that when a pilot made his solo flight, a piece of his shirt was ripped off and his name was printed on it. This scrap of memory was then hung at the airport of the flight. Gardner Birch had a more permanent

Corporate planes hangared at the airport brought extra income. Cooper-Bessemer's Cessna 195 is in front while Montgomery's Navion is in the back right.

Established in '38, the Grove City Diner across from the college was THE local hangout.

memento in mind and possibly a marketing tool to sell flying lessons. He created five plywood boards (19.5 inches wide and 45.5 inches high) that would list the names and solo dates of the students trained under his management. Names and dates are uniformly scripted in black paint (probably by a sign painter). Five boards list 127 students, starting in May of '44 through July of '48. Fifteen of them are women, including the first solo student, Helen J. Arnold, and they now hang at the current Grove City Airport.

81

Solo Board 1

HELEN J. ARNOLD	MAY·17·1944
FRANCIS T. STEPHENS	MAY·22·1944
KARL R. MEDROW	MAY·23·1944
CLARENCE E. RODGERS	MAY·24·1944
ROBERT F. McGOWAN	MAY·31·1944
BETTY J. McCORD	JUN·8·1944
RICHARD P. WALTERS	JUN·11·1944
FRED BECHTEL	JUN·15·1944
H. CRAIG SHIRA	JUL·9·1944
HAROLD R. BRYDON	JUL·13·1944
JAMES P. KELLY	JUL·15·1944
HILLES G. KEMP	JUL·16·1944
RAYMOND C. CORNELIUS	JUL·20·1944
MARY L. DAVIS	JUL·23·1944
ARTHUR R. McBRIDE	AUG·3·1944
ROY C. McCLUSKEY JR.	AUG·19·1944
JEAN T. HOGUE	AUG·26·1944
GORDON LEFEBVRE	SEP·1·1944
HAROLD L. RENICK	SEP·2·1944
BERTHA E. MUELLER	SEP·6·1944
EVELYN F. KREIDLE	SEP·8·1944
CLIFFORD C. GILLS	SEP·9·1944
JOHN I. THOMPSON	SEP·16·1944
ELEANOR E. WILLIAMSON	OCT·7·1944
JOHN L. THOMPSON	OCT·8·1944
RALPH E. RICE	OCT·12·1944
RICHARD L. BAGNALL	OCT·16·1944

Everyone at the airport called Gardner Birch simply "Birch." Nicknames were common. Dick Double, one of Birch's students, recalls, "I would say that your father did 90 percent of his instructing with three words: 'Follow me through!' That is, you (the student) placed your hands and feet on the dual controls, then Birch would fly the aircraft through the maneuver using his controls. Then he would say, 'Your turn.' The student, by feel, and with his own controls, would then simulate what your dad had just done."

Joe Susi, a life-long instructor, recalls the training structure in J-3 Cubs during the '40s. "The first flight lesson would be something in the order of the following. The instructor would take the aircraft up to about 2,500 feet of altitude in the practice area. Here, the student would get to actually control the airplane, working on straight and level, turns, climbing, descending. At this altitude, one could make some mistakes and there would be time for a correction to normal flight. An altimeter and air speed indicator on the front panel helped with these corrections. During this flight, the concern will be altitude, attitude and heading. Altitude is height in feet. Attitude is level wings, level nose, nose up, nose down. Heading is the direction we are going with a magnetic compass."

Joe continued, "The student would see the attitude by matching parts of the airplane to the natural horizon (there are no gyroscopic indicators in the Cub). You would be flying by the sight picture, using your eyes, your ears (vestibular sense of balance from the inner ear canals), the 'feel' of things (proprioceptor kinesthesia). This is that old bit about 'flying by the seat of your pants.'

As you proceeded with your training, other things would be covered: stalls, spins, traffic pattern, take-off, landing, go-arounds, wind correction maneuvers, emergency procedures. Then you would solo. The instructor would be watching you from the ground. Congratulations!"

A student had a suggested eight hours of dual instruction before being ready for his first solo. Fred "Posy" Thompson, one of the airport regulars, articulates this so well. "A good instructor knows within an hour or so when a student is ready to leave the ranks of the Dodo birds (a clumsy, flightless extinct bird). Therefore the instructor watches for an opportune moment to free his student from the 'surly bonds' (from the poem 'High Flight' by John Gillespie Magee Jr.). Usually when a student is ready to solo and makes a bad landing, it is a propitious time to send him off alone. On the taxi back to the take-off point, the instructor feigns fear and anger and tells the student to 'Stop!' Now the instructor opens the door and throws his hat out in anger and disgust, unbuckles his seatbelt, (but buckles it and leaves it on the seat), climbs out and informs the student, 'I have a wife and three kids and I'm afraid to ride with you. So make three take-offs and landings, hopefully better than the last! This sort of thing was done to keep the 'hot rocks' from being over-confident and making a fatal error. NOW! The student confronts the great empty space once occupied by his guide and mentor. The moment of truth is upon him. After checking everything 15 times and making sure no planes are on final approach, he slowly advances the throttle to wide open, the tail quickly comes up, and for the first time he has an unobstructed view of the runway. The aircraft, no longer burdened by the weight of the instructor, leaps into the air and, much to the student's surprise, climbs like crazy. Time to make adjustments. His position in the pattern is much different when solo. He reaches 400 feet and time for the first turn, so fast the airplane is getting ahead of him. This is his first acquaintance with the ever-changing adjustments a pilot must make. Training takes over and he arrives on the downwind, opposite the touch-down point. Carburetor heat is applied and the throttle is slowly closed, and a 60-mile-an-hour glide is set up. Every couple of minutes, a blast of the throttle is applied to keep the engine from loading up so that power will be available if needed. He makes a faultless landing known among his peers as a 'greaser.' After a second good landing, often the third one is a poor one and he is glad his solo is over. Shirttail cut off and signed by his instructor, or his name painted on a board: it doesn't matter. Like those who have gone before him, he has just experienced that he has much to learn."

If a student continued after his solo toward a Private Pilot Certificate, he or she would need a total time of 40 hours, of which 20 hours would be dual instruction. Part of this was night flight training going cross-country. Many small airport runways, including Grove City, were not lighted. Lanterns or car headlights were used to outline the landing strip after dark. Training flights, and then cross-country flights, were done first with the instructor then ultimately alone—totally alone, as a Piper Cub had no radio equipment. Ten hours of solo flying were required including the solo cross-country of at least 100 miles.

Corwin Meyer, Grumman test pilot in WWII, knew the drill. "If you aren't sweating too much before a flight, you surely haven't asked enough questions. If you are not sweating just a little during the flight, you may not be attentive enough. And, if you are not sweating out the answers with all the experts you can think of after the flight, you may never find that very beautiful pearl in all that pig litter."

Clarence Eugene "Gene" Rodgers spent his teen years in the mid-1930s in a Civilian Conservation Corps work camp. The CCC, one of Roosevelt's New Deal programs, was designed to put jobless young men to work in national forests, on federal conservation efforts and on road construction projects. The resulting CCC work camps were run by the U.S. Army. Single men between the ages of 18 and 25 who were healthy, unemployed and without financial resources received $30 a month, room and board, and health care. Armed with pickaxes, shovels, saws and their own muscles, these CCC boys sowed grass, planted trees, fought forest fires, cut hiking trails and built everything from bridges to public swimming pools. In the nine years it existed, the CCC helped 2.9 million youngsters learn about conservation as well as the skills to practice it.

Gene returned from the CCC and became a machinist at Cooper-Bessemer, "and a darn good one," according to Bill Raymer. Bill was a classmate of Gene's sister and brother, and a career Cooper-Bessemer employee. Gene went into the Navy in '42 or '43 and, with his Cooper-Bessemer training, worked in the engine room of an aircraft carrier in the South Pacific. Planes and adventure got in his blood. Upon discharge he used his GI benefits for

A young Gene Rodgers, front row, center, sits in his Navy whites.

lessons at the airport. He soloed on May 24, 1944. In a 1993 Experimental Aircraft Association interview, Gene recalls that day. "It had been raining a lot and the grass field had dips in it. My instructor told me I could do it. I took off. On the descent, I leaned out the left window, landing in a big puddle with water spraying all over my face. I was told to do it again; this time without a problem. I was on my own from there. We didn't have radios then, just detailed sectional maps. One Sunday a father asked me to take him to Wooster, Ohio, to see his daughter in college. I was using my compass and got to the Canfield Race Track okay, but then I couldn't pinpoint landmarks. At one point I saw a big field with a house next to it. I landed and walked up to the door. A man opened it and said 'Where did you come from?' I asked him to show me on the map where his house was. I was nine miles north of Wooster." Good common sense and self-reliance were a must for pilots in those days.

Raymer, who owned two planes with Gene, (a Piper Cherokee and Aeronca Chief 85-horsepower) remembers what a daredevil his friend was at times. The Aeronca, on its dashboard, stated, "Do not spin this aircraft." Gene was flying one day with Bill, and Bill remembers, "Holy cats! Next thing I knew we were in a spin AND a loop! (In a spin recovery, a good bit of speed was built up which could be used to do a loop). This was a wild and woolly guy, but smart. He could do almost anything."

Gene's brother, Jim, tells more about the wilder side. "Gene loved to do aerobatics. Once some people were picnicking at a steeplechase. Gene swooped down so low, people went diving to hide under anything. Another time he was flying near Emlenton. The bridge there goes across the Allegheny River—he flew right under the bridge!" Gene Rodgers was an accomplished pilot who could relate to the following verse by an unknown author:

> *Our pilots do a lot of stunts,*
> *And do them well of course,*
> *And if you think that isn't hard,*
> *Just try to loop your horse.*

Bob McGowan took his first flying lesson in Ohio at age 15. By age 17, he had had several instructors, "but Birch was the best instructor I ever had," he said. "After a number of dual hours together, he told me 'Stop. I want you to take it around yourself. Remember, my weight isn't there. You're going to float more.' I was very nervous!" That was on May 31, 1944 (Birch's 34th birthday). "I then started flying those yellow J-3 Cubs all over the country." In November 1945, Bob was drafted into the Army for 19 months. He did some plane maintenance and was a control tower operator for six months. As an adult, he earned his commercial and instrument rating licenses. He flew his own plane many hours for his business travel. "I never had anything serious happen, I never made the headlines."

Little is known about the later years of Betty J. "BJ" McCord. But Birdy Mueller remembers her as avant-garde and way ahead of her time. It's not surprising that this brown-haired feminist "did

her thing" and soloed on June 8, 1944.

H. Craig Shira, a local pharmacist with his own drug store in Grove City, soloed on July 9, 1944.

In direct contrast to all the young students, Harold Brydon was 40 years old and a business man when he began his flying. He owned both the Ferris Coal Co. and the Harold Brydon Coal Co. and lived in Slippery Rock. He soloed on July 13, 1944, and earned a private license. Within a year or two, one of his large belt shovels at a strip mine needed a new "crowd chain." Coal couldn't be loaded. Harold decided to save time and fly to Wisconsin to pick it up. He went out to the Grove City Airport and rented a twin-engine plane. After picking up the chain, he barely cleared some wires at the end of the Wisconsin airport on his takeoff. He had calculated the weight of the chain, but someone hadn't added in the weight of the pallet and packing materials. Not long after, he was talking to his insurance agent, who explained that if something had happened to him on that business trip, he would not have been covered. His insurance was for private flight. Harold, with his maturity, weighed his choices and risks and never flew again.

Hillis Kemp said, "It was just something I wanted to do, I had no fear." He started taking flying lessons in high school in Belmont, Ohio. In November 1943, he was drafted into the Navy. After boot camp, he was stationed at Grove City College's Navy Electronics School for four months. "I had had a student's pilot license for three years and had several different instructors with 12 hours of dual time before I soloed. Birch checked me out for my solo one Sunday afternoon

IF DUAL		INSTRUMENT RADIO-HOOD LINK.	SOLO		REMARKS OR CERTIFICATION	TOTAL TIME
AS INSTRUCTOR	AS STUDENT		NIGHT	DAY		
	6:20					6:20
	50				Stalls - Spins - Landings Y.R.B. #66923	7:10
	50				Take-offs Landings - Solo Y.R.B. #66923	8:00
	30			30	Take-off Landings Series	8:30
	20			20	Rect. Stalls. S - Turns	8:50
	10			15	Landings	9:05
	15				Dual check-out - Landings Y.R.B. #66923	9:20
				20	Take off Landings	9:40
				30	Rect. Takeoff - Landing Series	10:10
				40	Turns - Take off - Landings	10:50
	20				Take Off - Landings	11:10
	30					11:40
					Raymond C Cornelius SIGNATURE OF PILOT	TOTAL TIME 11:40

PUBLISHED AND COPYRIGHTED BY TRADER AERO SUPPLY, PITTSBURGH, PA.

Ray Cornelius logs his flight time.

(July 16, 1944). He was flying passengers in a red Super Cruiser. Out of nowhere, he came flying along side of me and waived me back to the airport. When we both landed, he told me I was flying too low over the town of Grove City." Solo back then was just that: no radio, no way to communicate, few instruments—pilots were on their own! "After that," Kemp said, "I was transferred to Chicago. I didn't have much money. My Navy pay was $70 a month, and dual instruction was $10 an hour. If I took a lesson, it was on a Sunday afternoon when I was off duty."

Ray Cornelius started as a line boy from June to September of 1943, at 50 cents an hour during the CPTP. It was a good summer job for a 16-year-old. When he graduated from high school the next year, he took the $45 he had received as graduation money and went out to the airport again. But this time it was to take lessons. "Birch was my teacher. I can remember, I was taking a lesson, the student always sat in the back. I was climbing too fast, and he banged his fist on the front of the plane and said, 'Keep the nose down, keep the nose down!' He was afraid I would stall out." In whirlwind time, Ray's life changed. Within a 10-day period in July of '44, he enlisted in the Navy, made his first solo and reported for active duty. On leave from boot camp in October, he went up alone, this time with his parents watching. "I landed in the crosswind. But I recovered. Your dad got on me because I hadn't looked at the windsock since taking off. Wind can change quickly. Two years later, after returning from the Navy, Birch stopped by to tell me I could take more lessons with the GI Bill. But I had decided to go to Grove City College instead."

The summer of 1944 was a notable time for the new, colorful CEO Gordon Lefebvre. Tall and distinguished, highly intelligent and always with a smile, he and Cooper-Bessemer had gained national prominence. He took pride that his company's production continued to boost war efforts. His career was flying, and so was he. Lefebvre lived the more conservative CEO role with his wife in Mt. Vernon, Ohio, but played it looser in Grove City. He pushed boundaries and took risks, but knew when not to go over the line. Gordon had several girlfriends whom he introduced as his daughters. Noted for his physical prowess, he could take a glass of whiskey and do a summersault while drinking it. Down to earth and showing no sign of his "station," he had the ability to relate to everyone and find a common bond. He could easily negotiate with powerful CEOs and politicians, then just as comfortably ask his shop people for their ideas and inquiries about their families.

Having kept the company Fairchild airplane at the airport for a year, Lefebvre felt comfortable there. The airport sat in the country by itself, and there he could be himself and let his wild side show. An old hand at sky escapades, he was now there for adventure. Gordon told this tall tale to the airport gang, including his instructor Birch and Bill Raymer. "Though born in Canada, Gordon goes to West Point. While there, he and three other cadets are assigned to go up in a tethered hot air balloon and draw maps of the surrounding countryside. The balloon broke loose and the next thing you know, they see the Atlantic Ocean! Somehow they land the balloon in a potato field owned by two old maids. The ladies take them in, and they have a good old time for two weeks until West Point

finds them and brings them back."

West Point records confirm that Gordon Lefebvre entered West Point Military Academy in 1908 as an Army Cadet, Class of 1912. West Point sits 50 miles north of New York City and is about 50 miles from the Atlantic Ocean, as the crow flies. Its role in history goes back to the Revolutionary War, and it is the oldest continuously occupied military post in America. Aware of the young country's need for engineers for development of railways, bridges, harbors and roads, West Point introduced civil engineering to its curriculum and made it the foundation. In post-Civil War times, West Point broadened its curriculum and became viewed as the first step in a continuing Army education. Gordon did not graduate from West Point, however, he may have known George Patton Jr. '09 or Omar Bradley and Dwight Eisenhower '15. Though he chose a corporate career over a military one, his affection and admiration for servicemen fighting in WWII was evident in his written remarks.

Lefebvre was the student, Birch the instructor—such a diverse pairing on the surface! Gordon had much more breadth to his worldly experiences at age 53, versus Birch at 34. Immense responsibility rested on his shoulders. Because Lefebvre was so busy, the two had an agreement that when Gordon found time for a lesson, Birch would give him priority. When the lesson was finished, he was onto his next appointment. Flying was still new and dangerous; a pilot's life was in his own hands and he better know what to do. An expert on reading people, Gordon would only give power to someone he trusted as the "best." Birch, mature beyond his years, matched and trumped him on responsibility as a teacher. He was serious and meticulous about all details and knew his stuff. Bill Raymer believes, "He was the smartest man I ever knew." From all accounts, the one thing Birch was not able to teach him was a smooth landing. Posy Thompson tells the story. "We'd be sitting in the office, hear a plane coming in for a landing, look out and see (hand undulates up and down) bump, bump, bump. Someone would say, 'Here comes Gordon.'"

Bertha "Birdy" Mueller was the office secretary and fellow student-pilot at the time. The girl that Lefebvre called "Peanut" remembers, "When Gordon soloed on September 1, 1944, he gave Gardner a very nice bonus, probably at least $100—a nice tidy sum for that day and age." (Hillis Kemp's Navy pay was $70 a month then.)

"Peanut" was from north of Pittsburgh. Her frugal parents had emigrated from Switzerland and bought a home in West View. Bertha "grew up there, then enrolled at Grove City College in September of 1943, as a secretarial student while there was a contingent of airmen training on campus." By the summer of '44, Birdy needed a job, and the airport needed a secretary. Besides, she had always been fascinated with airplanes and wanted to learn how to fly. She often took the local bus to work. In September 2006, Birdy found a paper she believes she had written for a college class, titled "Duties of the Aviation Secretary in 1944-45, Grove City Airport, Grove City, Pa." It included:

●Keep records of all money coming in. Sources: Payment for student lessons. The rate differed for dual or solo time. Payment of 10 hours in advance allowed for an 11th hour free. Each student's time had to be credited to an instructor's account for commission purposes.

●Gasoline purchases made by cross-country pilots visiting from other airports. (Sometimes I even had to pump gas if I was the only one available.)

●Sale of log books, candy incidentals. (This involved petty cash.)

●Coke and cigarette machines. (Cigarettes were hard to come by during the war and we only received "generic," i.e. unknown brands for the machine. Consequently, very few packs got into the machine but were rationed between the smokers—of which there were many.)

●In September of '44, Fin Wilson purchased a bi-winged WACO for the purpose of giving rides to interested customers—I collected the money.

●Deposit money in night depository at bank.

●Every two weeks, do payroll, i.e. figure number of hours per employee. Employees included instructor, maintenance and clerical personnel.

●Keep record of each airplane's time in the air in addition to each hour that engine was running, i.e. two logbooks per aircraft. (Engines were switched between aircraft as they were repaired and maintained.)

●All gas sales and usage had to record the NC number of the aircraft (now an N number), kind of engine, horsepower of engine and purpose for which the gas was used: lessons (solo and dual), pleasure, business, etc. Many of these regulations were mandated by the Office of Price Administration (OPA).

●Complete forms required by the CAA. When a student soloed, the student's test of Civil Air Regulations had to be sent to them with a form in triplicate giving details of the flight: length, weather, time of day, number of landings, etc.

●At the end of each month, summary sheets had to be sent to the OPA and bills had to be sent to customers who bought gas on credit or stored their aircraft in the hangar. Also, a record had to be sent to the insurance company giving the exact amount of time each airplane flew during the month.

●Maintain files, distribute mail, complete government forms, answer phone, handle inquiries by visitors, fill Coke machine, dispense first aid, etc.

Birdy, continues, "A three-word job description: 'Whatever it took.' I worked five afternoons a week as I had lab classes the other two days. Professor Russell Smith held ground school classes two nights a week at the airport, each session was three hours long for 12 weeks. The four ground school courses required to complete a private license were: Airplanes and Engines, Meteorology, Civil Air Regulations and Navigation. The student would then take a written test on these subjects."

With all the above, there was still time for Birdy to study on the job. By paying in advance and with an employee discount, on July 25, 1944, she could finally afford those "dreamed of" lessons. With amazing speed, she soloed five days after Gordon, on September 6. Birdy remembers, "I felt like I was ready, I was excited." On a bone-chilling January 9, 1945, she checked out in a Cub equipped with skis. By January 25 she was ready

Birdy Mueller gets ready to fly on Easter 1945. Oh, what a feminine pilot!

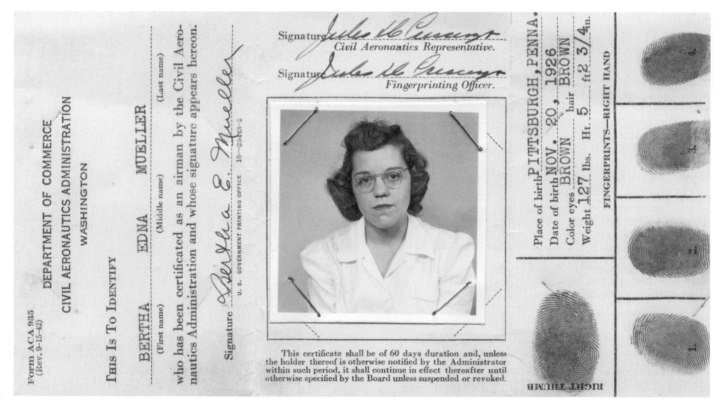

Birdy Mueller is certified as an airman by the CAA.

for her first cross-country with Fuzzy. Finally, as recorded in her log book, on August 12, 1945, she took her private flight test under Fin Wilson.

Another rare female pilot, Evelyn Kreidle, recalls, "I don't know why we decided to take flying lessons, wish I could make up some glamorous reason, it was probably a dare." Evelyn and Eleanor Williamson were both students at the college and friends. John Kreidle, Evelyn's dad, worked at Cooper-Bessemer as an assemblyman. Studying to be a business teacher, she had also worked at Cooper-Bessemer a summer earlier, typing time sheets. For whatever reason, now not remembered by Evelyn, she and Eleanor took the challenge! Often the pair rode their bikes to the airport. Evelyn paid for her lessons with baby-sitting money. Because normally she got very car sick, she even surprised herself. Flying didn't bother her, not the loops, stalls or spins. "I remember the first time your father took me up in the plane. I was thinking as we climbed, it's too far from land. But after I was flying for a time, I kept thinking that the ground was too close and I wanted to go higher. My most vivid memory of your father was his repeating (the same phrase) every time I was to land, 'If you think you are down far enough, you aren't.' That must have been ingrained in my mind, because after many landings, I realized I was down far enough and didn't have to go down further. On the day I soloed, after practicing landings, (Birch) had me land the plane and said to me, 'I forgot my pen in the office.' He got out and I thought to myself, 'He's letting me solo.' And I took off, unafraid!" That was September 8, 1944, just a few days before she went off for her first teaching job in Olean, N.Y.

A receipt for Evelyn Kreidle shows a discount for flying lessons paid in advance.

Once there, the cost to get to the airport was too much; she had to give up flying.

Two blocks separated the Kreidle and Williamson homes, the latter built by Eleanor's grandfather. Both girls were living at home while attending college and both were majoring in business education. Eleanor still has a mind for figures. "I paid $9 for a half hour for flight instruction. Though I was apprehensive when it came time to solo, I knew that Birch thought I was ready or he wouldn't have let me go. It was very exciting and I did fine. My mother used to say that I'd fly over the house and tip the wing." She added about 35 total hours to her logbook, then was pulled in another direction. Her father set her up in business before Christmas of 1945 as co-owner of the El-Gra Fashion dress shop on Broad Street. She was finishing her senior year as well. Just 21 years old, yet she could have been the "We can do it!" poster-girl for new women that the war had created. Twenty-seven students were noted on Board 1, and seven were thoroughly modern '40s women. But they were not unique.

The development of wartime economy had given women more freedom than they had ever had before. For the first time, women were able to experience some sort of social and economic mobility; they were able to explore their own individuality and independence. At the end of 1943, one-third of war workers were women. The demands put on American industry by the war machine were immense. With some 10 million men at war and the rest of the male population at work, it was clear the only way America would be able to win the war was if it enlisted large numbers of women for employment. America needed its women to go to work to build the planes, tanks and ships needed to fight Hitler. World War II, more than any other war, was a war based on production, and so it was time to bring American women into industry. The emotional appeal of patriotism and the idea of increased economic prosperity were used to lure women into the workforce. They were constantly reminded that their husbands, sons and brothers were in danger because they were not receiving the supplies they needed. Slogans such as "Victory is in your hands," "We can do it" and "Women, the war needs you!" were all used to convince women that their country's needs were more important than their individual comfort. As a result of the propaganda, in July 1944, when war was at its peak, more than 19 mil-

lion women were employed in the United States, more than ever before.

More than two million women found themselves in every aspect of the war industry: making military clothing, operating hydraulic presses, building fighter planes, serving as volunteer firefighters. American women worked day and night; one-third of women war workers were mothers of children living at home. And when they got home, they washed clothes in wringer washing machines and hung them on an outdoor clothesline. They ironed all clothes by hand. Laundry often took an entire day. Childcare facilities were lacking, and food was cooked from rationed ingredients a meal at a time. The only thing fast about food was the speed at which it was eaten. Mother cleaned up the dishes, bathed and put the kids to bed, then cleaned a little. Men still had very limited roles in the day-to-day duties of the home. And many were away at war. Women took on multiple roles that created many different feelings about this new phase of their life.

Eleanor Roosevelt, the epitome of the modern, independent woman, wrote in Reader's Digest in January 1944, "Our women are serving actively in many ways in this war, and they are doing a grand job on both the fighting front and the home front. Commanding officers feel that the women in our military services have performed their duties more efficiently than the men whom they have freed for active service. So far, WACs (Women's Army Corps) have been the only ones allowed overseas. The restriction on the activities of our other women's military services is due to a false chivalry, which insists that women be protected from war hazards and hardships, even against their own wishes. I think this idea of sheltering women is a shortsighted policy, since one of the great post-war difficulties will be the readjustment of men and women who have been long separated. That adjustment will be easier if both have experienced a similar discipline and acquired a similar attitude toward life."

Mrs. Roosevelt would have opened up the military to women pilots. "We are in a war and we need to fight it with all our ability and every weapon possible. Women pilots, in this particular case, are a weapon waiting to be used." But opposition ran deep. The best compromise achieved under Hap Arnold was WASP: Women Air Force Service Pilots, headed by Jackie Cochran and Nancy Harkness Love. WASP delivered 12,650 needed aircraft and flew 60 million miles to key locations, freeing up male pilots for front-line duty. At the cost of personal and professional sacrifices, 12,000 WASPs played an integral part in winning the war in the air as unofficial pilots for the United States Army Air Force. Posy has high regard. "These ladies flew any and all of the hairy-chested war planes of WWII. Even the Martin B-26: 'The Baltimore Whore,' so called because of the very short wings (no visible means of support). I guess it was something to behold when the WASPs delivered a B-26 to an operational squadron and two dainty females climbed out." These females provided not only critical equipment, but a brief uplift of morale.

"Many thousands of women are not doing any unusual work, but are simply running their houses quietly and efficiently, are contributing more to the war effort than they themselves realize," the vocal Eleanor Roosevelt wrote. "The woman who meets war difficulties with a smile, who does her best with rationing and other curtailments, who writes her man overseas the kind of letters he must have to carry him successfully, is making a great contribution to this difficult period. If, in addition to this work at home, a woman is giving her services to any of the volunteer organizations, our hats must be off to her. Undoubtedly there are some women who are leading the same sort of life today that they have always led; but I think they must be having a difficult time finding companionship. For the vast majority of women in this country, life has changed. Their thoughts and hearts are concerned with what is happening in countless places in the world. They are only content as they feel they are contributing something toward the speedier ending of the war and a better chance for their men in the world in the future." American women in all walks of life exhibited a mix of fortitude and boldness as they stepped into their rightful place and contributed fully to the war effort.

With a head of gorgeous red hair, John "Jack" Thompson graduated from Grove City High School and had just enough time in the summer to squeeze in flying lessons before he was shipped out to war. His widow, Dorothy, who fondly calls him "Red," remembers, "Fuzzy was his instructor, but he thought the world of Birch. Birch, jolly and always laughing, took me up in an open cockpit plane and almost scared me to death." Jack soloed on October 8, 1944, and was drafted almost immediately into the Army's engineer corps. He served in Japan, was trained to run heavy equipment and helped to build the Dakota Air Strip there. When he returned home, he married Dorothy in 1946. Jack went to work for the Bobo Stripping Company as a drag line operator and still managed to do some occasional flying.

Solo Board 2

GEORGE O. HOOVER	OCT·29·1944
JAMES B. DALY	NOV·11·1944
CHARLES J. DICKEY	DEC·4·1944
NORMAN H. LATSHAW	JAN·14·1945
JAMES R. DOWLING	MAR·8·1945
BYRON ROBEY	APR·8·1945
EMIL E. MEIER	APR·10·1945
ROBERT C. ALRICH	APR·17·1945
JOHN E. CREIGHTON	MAY·6·1945
MERL A. NEWELL	MAY·30·1945
RICHARD G. MOON	JUN·3·1945
JOHN B. NEEL	JUN·19·1945
RAY W. DUNKERLEY	JUN·29·1945
L. RICHARD HOLSTINE	JUN·30·1945
MURIEL D. NELSON	JUL·13·1945
DONALD H. BRINER	AUG·5·1945
WILLIAM A. DAVIS	AUG·7·1945
FRANCIS E. CAMPBELL	AUG·17·1945
ALBERT C. MYERS	AUG·18·1945
EDITH E. KINDER	AUG·27·1945
ROBERT E. WALTHOUR	AUG·27·1945
WILLIAM H. KOENIG	AUG·30·1945
MARGARET L. ROSSMAN	SEP·12·1945
N. DARRELL HASSEL	SEP·15·1945
DOROTHY E. CAMPBELL	OCT·3·1945
RICHARD A. MACKELL	OCT·3·1945
RALPH E. BROWN	OCT·11·1945

Board 2

Autumn leaves had fallen, all was decorated for Halloween and every child could tell you what costume he or she would wear. Dr. George Hoover was a new intern at Bashline Rossman Osteopathic Hospital and Clinic in Grove City, having just graduated in late spring from the Philadelphia School of Osteopathic Medicine. He had always wanted to fly, so he went to the airport, talked to the instructors and began taking lessons from Birch. Dr. Hoover recounts, "On the day I soloed (October 29, 1944), after we had a dual lesson and landed, Birch said, 'Stop here, I want to check the tail wheel.' He got out, buckled his seatbelt (a safety issue if left unbuckled), and he said, 'Get out of here!' Flying was expensive, and when I got married in 1946, my wife was unhappy with it, so I stopped."

Born in 1919 and raised on a 140-acre farm in Slippery Rock, Chuck Dickey and his brother Elmer were farming it alone when the war broke out. According to Dickey, "Someone from the draft board came out to the farm and said with authority, 'One of you is going into the Army, and the other can run the farm. Now flip a coin.' Elmer lost the coin toss and went to the service, returning when the war was over. When the airport advertised they were giving lessons (to civilians), I went out and took lessons. I was there when Birdy soloed, and said 'if that dainty lady can do it, I can too.' Fuzzy was my instructor. I soloed on December 4 (1944). Winters were much worse then, with a lot of snow. One or two of the Piper Cubs were equipped with plywood skis, and I flew on skis."

The most memorable event in his life to take place in the air occurred on April 14, 1945. Handsome Chuck in a blue pinstripe suit married his pretty sweetheart Marie McCurdy, wearing a stylish powder blue dress with white rose corsage, at 2,000 feet over the Dickey farm. It was Fuzzy's idea that Chuck combine his two great loves, Marie and flying. Fuzzy served as pilot. Rev. William Riddle, pastor of three rural churches, was there to perform the ceremony. According to the society page, "The four climbed into a red and blue WACO QDC cabin plane at 4:40 p.m. Gardner Birch spun the propeller and the ship whisked off into the low-hanging clouds. Half an hour later, the knot firmly tied, they landed and taxied to the hangar. Friends waiting at the office threw rice as they stepped out of the plane, exhilarated by the ceremony. Now down to earth, they were in a hurry to leave for a reception being held at 6:00 at the bride's parents' home."

The calendar page hanging at the airport read December 1944. Winter air was seeping through the cracks and under the huge hangar doors that weren't being opened very often. Harsh weather produced little flight revenue. While it was quiet and slow at the airport, activity connected to the war was at an all-time high. The manpower demand was relentless and desperate. Within the next six months, there would be 12 million people in the U.S. Armed Forces and more than 400,000 dead or missing in action; and several times that were wounded. Combat casualties surged beyond all expectations. About 10 million were drafted; the rest had enlisted. Voluntary enlistment, which let one choose the service one wished to join, had stopped in '43. The Armed Forces was running out of men. Looking back, Jerome Peppers stated, "We used our manpower unwisely and could have been in serious manning problems in the war production and military service had the war not gone so well for us. Fortunately ... the war ended before unwise manpower ... policies could

Newlyweds Come Down To Earth

Landing at Grove City Airport after being married up in "the wide blue yonder" are Mr. and Mrs. Charles Dickey of Slippery Rock, in the back seat. Rev. William Riddle and Pilot Murl DeArment also got a kick out of it.

Slippery Rock Couple Married In Air Over Their Farm Homes

Charles Dickey And Marie McCurdy Are Principals In Unusual Ceremony

Charles Dickey, 25, loves J. Marie McCurdy, 21—and airplanes.

So he married her late Saturday afternoon 2,000 feet above their farm homes near Slippery Rock.

The bridegroom soloed for the first time Dec. 4 at Grove City Airport. Murl DeArment, his instructor, co-manager of the field, suggested the idea of combining his student's two chief interests and the latter thought it was a swell idea. Miss McCurdy had no

(Continued on Page Eight, Col. 3)

Chuck and Marie Dickey fly into marriage.

return to bite us … we really had no effective plan for the full-scale manpower mobilization which was required.

"To reach the number needed, about 45 million men between the ages of 18 and 45 registered for the draft. About 31 million were found physically and mentally qualified. But there were many draft deferments for individuals in both agriculture and essential war industries. Many others had deferments, too: civil servants, hardship cases, religious officials, aliens, conscientious objectors, handicapped people, fathers, etc. Too many deferred men led the War Manpower Commission to issue a list of 'nondeferable' occupations and call on draft boards to reclassify such people to 1-A category. The 6,500 separate draft boards, under the independent Selective Service, refused. Congress also disagreed with many of the Commissions edicts too. Too many agencies, levels of bureaucracies and too much politics. In April '44, Selective Service ordered that men with dependents be reclassified, and in July it was apparent that fathers would have to be taken in the near future. In December '44, James F. Byrnes, head of War Mobilization (then later Secretary of State under Harry Truman), issued the 'Work or Fight Order.' His purpose was to drive men up to age 38, either into essential jobs that were unpopular or into the service." National orders were in place to ensure manpower needs, but what would local draft board do about them? Who would be called up to finish the war?

With airport business at a near standstill and a frigid long winter ahead, Birch and Fuzzy had plenty of time to think about their situation. Both were fathers (Birch had three children, Fuzzy one) under 38. They had loved training the cadets under the CPTP and had felt a strong sense of war purpose, but they lost their exempt status with the CPTP disbandment in May. If they were drafted, in all realty, their positions at the airport would be filled and unavailable when they came home. Did they want to take that chance? They had another choice.

Gordon Lefebvre had a huge soft spot in his heart for the airport and the men there, especially Birch and Fuzzy. As CEO of Cooper-Bessemer, he was in the position to offer them exempt status jobs on the 3 to 11 p.m. shift. And this is how they answered the potential "work or fight" draft issue: days at the airport, war-production work in the evening—working two jobs to save the one they really wanted. No one ever said that war has easy answers.

They survived the long hours and had the maturity to know it was short-term. Fuzzy lived in Grove City. But Gardner lived in Hickory, 30 miles to the west. Some nights he slept on a cot at the airport rather than drive home. War restrictions limited driving speed to 35 miles per hour and gas was rationed. Sometimes weather was a problem. But they made it work.

In the spring of 1945, Cooper-Bessemer got an order from the Navy for six tail hooks for fighters. Cooper-Bessemer hired Wilson Aviation to deliver them to a military base in Kentucky as soon as possible. Gardner Birch was to fly the red and blue bi-plane '30s WACO and the cargo to its destination. Bill Raymer relays these events: "Your dad flew into the wrong restricted military airfield and had a hard time getting out! He had no authority (security clearance), and they had to make phone calls and check him out. But he could talk his way out of anything. Then he flew on to the correct field, not far away." Birch was normally very precise. How could he have missed the correct base?

"Remember, he was flying with minimal instruments for direction. Back then, you used a map, a compass and a watch for 'line of site navigation.' You would draw a line (your route) on a map, take a paper protractor and check your course. You are relying on speed, time and fuel. Your compass, mounted on the instrument panel, was not stable and wobbled around, giving a magnetic course but not a true course. Wind can affect your speed. You have to rely on checkpoints on you map (which you cross-hatched), such as railroad tracks, high peaks and water towers for visual guidance. You had to be able to see the ground for confirmation. Bad weather could be a problem. The airfields were located in the same area, they were hard to see at the same time. He got confused and landed at the wrong one. They looked similar on the map and on the ground. He had quite an adventure."

Fred "Posy" Thompson comments on "Willie" Raymer's explanation. "His statement is essentially correct. Navigation was by speed, time and distance. Wind drift was the culprit and it complicated most flights. Don't feel bad about your father landing at the wrong airport. Modern airliners with their myriad and expensive instruments have been known to land at the wrong airport."

Few Americans were aware of President Roosevelt's health struggles in the spring of '45, though rumors ran wild. His haggard and weak appearance was due to heart ailments, high blood pressure and bronchitis. The strain of his election victory for a fourth term over Thomas E. Dewey in November '44 and then the Yalta Conference in February '45 took their toil. Churchill, Stalin and FDR had fashioned arrangements for a post-war Europe at Yalta, and it resulted in the formation of The United Nations. In April, FDR returned to his favorite healing retreat in Warm Springs, Ga. There on April 12, while sitting for a portrait, he collapsed and died of a cerebral hemorrhage. Vice President Harry S. Truman took the oath of office the same day. But even more significant were the deaths of two other world leaders.

In Europe, the Red Army began its final assault on Berlin on April 16. Hitler and his staff moved into a concrete bunker beneath the Chancellery. Events snowball. On April 21, the Soviets reach Berlin. On April 28, Mussolini was captured and hanged, and the Allies took Venice. On April 29, the U.S. 7th Army liberated Dachau. On April 30, Hitler committed suicide. By May 2, German troops in Italy had surrendered. On May 7, there was unconditional surrender of all German forces to Allies. May 8 was declared Victory in Europe Day (V-E Day). Half the war was over.

Those events lifted an uncertain cloud from the airport and sparked an increase in lessons. John Creighton was still in high school and dreamed of becoming a pilot. To that end, he rode his bike to the airport and took lessons. Birch sent him off on his solo on May 6, 1945, with John knowing he could do it. Even 60 years later, he remembers this fine hour. Shortly after his solo, he took his father, who had never been in a plane before, for a ride. "He was so proud of me!" John recounts. In the next months, he went to college, then into the military — first a try for the Air Force, but ending up as a Marine. He didn't become a pilot, but became a hero in his dad's eyes.

In contrast to John Creighton was Johnny Neel. On his 17th birthday, June 1, 1943, he signed up with the Marines. He was on an aircraft carrier, the USS Wasp, in the South Pacific as a gunner until '45. Coming home, he was intent on becoming a pilot. He used his wages from working for a coal company and then his GI benefits to take lessons, soloing on June 19, 1945. He first earned a student pilot license, then a private license, then a commercial pilot certificate along with special pilot ratings—a minimum of 200 hours. Lessons and plane rentals were expensive and the time involved turned into eight years. But he persisted.

The commercial rating required one hour of controllable propeller time. The flight school had no such plane. Fred "Posy" Thompson was now a regular part of the airport gang. Having taken lessons on the GI Bill elsewhere, Posy happened upon a deal to buy a surplus military aircraft (a Consolidated-Vultee BT-13A) for $500. "This ship had only 50 hours on a new P&W engine and a Hamilton Standard propeller. Your father asked if I would allow the use of my new BT so that his students could get the required one hour. We agreed that for every hour flown, he would replace the gas used and add another 25 gallons.

Birch traded Posy 25 gallons of free gas for each hour's use of his $500 Consolidated-Vultee BT-13A.

This was a good deal because gas was cheap back in those days and, money-wise, it would amount to about $9 an hour to use my airplane. I was happy to get the gas and the guys got their one-hour requirement. The only trouble was if they shot landings and take-offs, gas consumption went to about 40 gallons per hour. Still, I didn't care as long as they didn't dig into my gas supply. But, I could not keep John Neel out of my airplane. The BT-13 didn't require a key, just turn on the master switch and magnetos to start the engine. But all flights were to be dual instruction flights. Even after I told him to leave it alone, he would still fly it. I even put a notice on the instrument panel that the plane was not airworthy. Did not make any difference, he flew it anyway. Your dad checked him and a lot of other people out in my ship." Johnny crossed lines but got results. In 1954, he began as a pilot for Eastern Airlines.

What would you be willing to do for flying lessons? Muriel "Dottie" Wood Nelson, married and 20 years old, was willing to ride her bike the couple miles to the airport for the privilege. Born and raised at 412 Memorial Avenue in Grove City, Dottie graduated from high school in '43. Her father, Patrick Wood, tested engines that Cooper-Bessemer built for Navy minesweepers. Dottie went to work there as an "inventory person." Making $.68 per hour, she had to count parts for engines. Dressed in a white blouse and black slacks, she was one of the first women to work in the shops of Cooper-Bessemer. It was an exciting time for her and she instinctively knew that new paradigms were being created in the workplace. She was working alongside men in an environment that accepted her efforts. This is a huge step forward in workplace equality for small-town Grove City.

Earning her own money, having had an interest in flying and having extra time while her husband was in the service, Dottie wanted those lessons after meeting Birch at Cooper-Bessemer. "I can still see those yellow planes lined up there. I was still young and crazy, I wasn't afraid. Your dad was a good instructor, but still we had a lot of fun and joked. He asked me if I knew east from west. I said 'the sun comes up on the east and sets in the west.' I soloed on July 13 of '45. I got to solo in an airplane before I owned a car!"

Dr. Don Briner had interned at Bashline Rossman Osteopathic Hospital and Clinic in Grove City and that's where he met his future wife, Betty, also an intern. According to Betty, "Don was an osteopathic physician for seven years in Mercer. He had a 2-A status during the war because he was the only doctor in the town. He had an itch to fly. I thought it was silly (and) was against it because of the safety issue. He had three kids! But he took lessons anyway while he was in practice (and soloed August 5, 1945). He was landing one time and the plane almost flipped over!" His doctor skills were much sharper than his pilot skills and much more needed.

Possibly because she had always been a tomboy and had seen the glamorous women pilots in the movies, Edith Kinder was intrigued by them. Her dad owned a garage and her mom had a grocery store in Barkeyville. They offered to pay for her flying lessons. Birch was her instructor. Although he had confidence and said, "You have come along so well, you're ready to solo," Edith was scared. "I'll never find my way back! But by following the roads and Route 8, I had a

good landing (on August 27, 1945). Then I knew. My instructor was right, I can do it!" Edith started a two-year college program and only flew off and on. But the confidence builder lasted a lifetime.

As summer ebbed, the war in the Pacific was coming to a head. The U.S. capture of islands such as Iwo Jima and Okinawa brought the Japanese homeland within range of naval and air attack. Dozens of cities were firebombed, including Tokyo, where 90,000 died. On August 6, 1945, the B-29 "Enola Gay" piloted by Col. Paul Tibbets dropped an atomic bomb (Little Boy) on Hiroshima, effectively destroying it. Two days later the Soviet Union declared war on Japan and launched a large-scale invasion of Japanese occupied Manchuria. The next day, August 9, the B-29 "Bock's Car," piloted by Maj. Charles Sweeney, dropped an atomic bomb (Fat Man) on Nagasaki. The combination of the use of atomic weapons and the new inclusion of the Soviet Union were both highly responsible for the unconditional surrender of Japan on August 14. On V-J (Victory Over Japan) Day, September 2, aboard the USS Missouri in Tokyo Bay, the Japanese signed official surrender papers.

Birdy "Peanut" Mueller had just flown with Fin for her private pilot certificate two weeks before this jubilant end to the war. Now was her chance to give a local version of a Hollywood style debut as a female pilot. In keeping with the significance of V-J Day, and in celebration, Grove City College cancelled all classes. Someone suggested going to the airport and renting a plane. Each of the girls got a waste paper basket and filled it with as much torn paper as they could find. Birdy was the pilot and, in her excitement, had to remember to keep an altitude of 500 feet above the city. The flying females, in a bright yellow Piper Cub with the famous black Z stripe, spread their homemade confetti over the city, creating a never-to-be-forgotten solo air parade to celebrate world peace. Birdy would say goodbye to the airport and her part-time job within days to enroll at Syracuse University. But her positive presence and energetic spirit would not be forgotten.

Aviation had an enormous impact on the course of the war, and war had just as significant an impact on aviation. Before 1938, there were 300 air transports in the U.S. By the end of the war, 40 manufacturers were producing 50,000 planes a year and the U.S. had 300,000 aircraft. Aircraft production had become the world's leading manufacturing industry. The manufacturing of fighters and bombers were a priority, but air transports kept people and supplies moving throughout the production chain while the war was fought at home.

Airlines now had more business than they could handle, both passengers and freight. While there were numerous advances in U.S. aircraft design during the war that enabled planes to go faster, higher and further than before, mass production was the chief goal domestically. The major innovations of radar and jet engines occurred in Europe.

World War II was a conflict that engulfed much of the globe and is considered the most costly and intense war in human history. It involved an overwhelming number of nations and an extraordinary number of theaters. About 50 million people died. Few areas of the world were unaffected; the war involved the "home front" and bombing of civilians to a new degree. Atomic

weapons, jet aircraft, rockets and radar, the massive use of tanks, submarines, torpedo bombers and destroyer and tanker formations are only a few of many wartime inventions and new tactics that changed the face of the conflict. The Allies (the Soviet Union, France, the United Kingdom, the U.S., China, Poland and more) were victors over the Axis (Germany, Japan, Italy, Romania, Hungary, Bulgaria and more).

The war was over, change was certain. Findley Wilson had shrewdly built Wilson Aviation by developing two very successful airports in New Castle and Grove City, and now he wanted more. He zeroed in on the Sharon area. This third leg of his triangular airport ownership would be in a more industrial, populated area. And, ironically, Gardner Birch lived there. In June of 1945, a 98.9-acre parcel of farm land off Route 18 from Hann Hill Road, south of Morefield Road in Hickory Township, went up for sheriff's sale. Michael and Bertha Lucas purchased it. It was large enough and in a good location for an airport. Fin wanted it. But it was not in his best interest to be known as the interested party at that time. He may have believed that his name would command a higher price. There was also word that he was involved in a law suit that required momentary anonymity on his part. Either way, he had Gardner Birch and his wife, Grace, enter into the contract and settle on the land on September 24, 1945. Fin fronted the purchase money. And 15 days later, Findley and Maxine Wilson purchased the same 98.9-acre piece of land from Gardner and Grace. Now there was a Sharon Airport. Fin created a grass runway, and the farmhouse served as the office. Birch lived just a mile from the airport and often commuted

Fin Wilson gets some free advertising for his airports thanks to Esso.

to Grove City by plane. Within three years, income from aviation services started to drop. Fin then leased the airport to Ed Chadderton, owner of Chadderton Trucking of Sharon. Ed grew up in Mercer, Pa., and started flying at the Mercer Airport in his early 20s. He had three and a half hours of instruction when he brought home a Cub Coupe and crashed into a pig pen on the family farm. Once the lease was in place with Fin, Ed built hangars, gave lessons through Chadderton Air Service, owned 17 airplanes at one time and even sponsored a Civil Air Patrol. Everyone local referred to it as "the Chadderton Airport"; no one knew it was a lease rather than an ownership interest (read more on page 143).

A childhood dream for Dick Mackell materialized. "As a boy living in Barkeyville, I was fascinated by the early mail planes, dropping bags of mail at selected sites, and picking up the mail bag hanging on a hook. They picked up in Grove City, then drove past my area to Franklin." This former Navy Commander is describing "skyhooking." In the 1930s, postal officials decided to test the feasibility of inaugurating airmail service in areas without adequate railway or highway mail links. The railway mail service's successful on-the-fly mail exchange system provided the inspiration for an aviation experiment. Mail would be hooked by a plane flying overhead and reeled up into the plane: not necessarily an easy task.

The plane that was initially used was a single-engine Stinson Reliant SR-10, capable of operating at speeds of 150 miles an hour. The crew consisted of the pilot and a flight officer who worked the pick-up mechanism, making the mail exchange. To deliver the mail, the flight officer lowered the nose-shaped cone container out of the bottom of the aircraft through a special opening. Almost at the same instant, an arm was lowered. The grappling hook snagged the hanging mail pouch suspended between a pair of 15-foot-high posts. Once the catch was made, the flight officer activated the winding mechanism to reel the mail canister into the plane. The method required great piloting skill and reliance on visual landmarks.

Beginning in May of 1939, All American Airways Company (later Allegheny Airlines and now US Airways) made 23,000 mail pickups this way, along two routes out of Pittsburgh and into Pennsylvania, Ohio, New York, Kentucky and West Virginia. The experimental routes covered 1,040 miles, served 150 post offices, picked up some 400,000 pieces of mail each month and lasted 10 years.

Dick Mackell continues, "In high school in Wesley, the principal taught a class that included a familiarization flight. We got to fly for about 10 minutes. It was always my intention to get my pilot's license. With the cost of lessons—$6 to solo, $9 for an instructor—it took me over two years, getting the money by hook or by crook. Finally I had eight hours, and under Gardner Birch I soloed on October 3, 1945. I was a senior and one month shy of 17. It was a big thrill and nothing went wrong. After graduation in June of '46, I signed up with the Navy and joined the Holloway Plan, a five-year program for aviation mid-shipmen. The first two years were at a college of your choice. I went to Grove City College and received a pay of $50 a month from the Navy while in general studies. Then I reported to Navy flight training."

Solo Board 3

WILLIAM K. MONG	OCT·17·1945
JAMES C. RODGERS	DEC·23·1945
C. GENE WILLIAMSON	JAN·16·1946
DAVID A. SCHMID	FEB·8·1946
THOMAS B. MARTIN	FEB·12·1946
RUSSELL DANNER	MAR·20·1946
RAYMOND W. FILER	MAR·28·1946
KENNETH W. SEFTON	APR·17·1946
JACK E. MARS	APR·29·1946
DANNY COMO	APR·30·1946
WILLIAM J. WEBSTER	MAY·1·1946
FRANCIS E. SEIPLE	MAY·6·1946
JAMES FASCETTI	MAY·15·1946
DONALD S. CORBETT	MAY·16·1946
JACK SCHMELTZER	MAY·16·1946
ROBERT C. HOCKENBERRY	MAY·16·1946
ARTHUR J. HEPLER	MAY·28·1946
VICTOR GUARNIERI	MAY·29·1946
JOHN W. KROFCHECK	MAY·29·1946
JOSEPH L. MATTHEWS	JUN·3·1946
HAROLD W. REED	JUN·14·1946
D. EDISON BLACK	JUN·15·1946
JOHN D. BARBER	JUN·22·1946
ARTHUR M. SHORTS	JUN·23·1946
WILLIAM J. RAYMER	JUL·12·1946
UNA ELLEN HART	JUL·13·1946
JOHN N. WELCH	JUL·13·1946

BOARD 3

In the small town of Wesley, Dick Mackell had a good friend — Bill Mong. They were in the same class and even formed a band together. Dick played drums, his sister Ellen was on the piano, and Bill played the trumpet. The band got together every Wednesday night and played at local churches, the Grange and other venues. Bill was bitten by the flying bug, driving a '36 Chevy to the airport for lessons. He, likewise, was not afraid when he soloed on October 17, 1945. The friends sometimes flew together, with Dick being the more adventurous. Once while piloting, Dick did two loops over a girlfriend's house. Sometimes, while flying Cubs with open doors, the two friends had mock dogfights. Bill was drafted into the Army in February of '46 and went into its radio school. Thirteen months later, he was discharged. Back at the corner diner, he ran into his flight instructors. While they asked him if he wanted to continue lessons under the GI Bill, he answered that he had instead decided to enroll at Grove City College to become an engineer.

Gene Rodgers' younger brother, Jim, had missed military duty because he had had polio as a child. But influenced by his big brother's passion for aviation, Jim thought it would be cool to take lessons, too. He progressed quickly. On a cold, blustery December 29, 1945, he had logged six or seven hours in his logbook, and snow was deep enough to require skis on the Piper Cub. He went up for dual instruction with Gardner Birch. Jim made a landing, and Birch excitedly said, "I have to shake the wing because these things (skis) freeze to the ground." Then he was given command to solo. Jim remembers, "I wondered what I was doing up there. But I landed on the skis; they make the smoothest landing because there is no bounce of the rubber tires. Another time I was up ready to land and overshot the runway. If I came down then, I'd have landed in the swamp. I had landed long and had to loop back toward the hangar. When I got back to the airport, I was told that I should have gone down sooner!" Students tended to fear the ground and unknowingly held back pressure on the stick. Posy says, "I had an instructor friend who told his student to 'Get your nose down!' repeatedly, but with no results. Finally he turned around to see the back of the student's head with his nose as near the floor as he could get it."

Rough winter weather continued. But when the calendar tells a potential pilot he or she is legal to solo, it's the day! David Schmid had been hitchhiking from Slippery Rock to the airport for more than a year to take lessons. Sometimes the wait for a passing car was an hour or more. But his $3 lawn mowing wages could pay for a 15-minute fly. The weather on his 16th birthday on February 8, 1946, was treacherous, with a ceiling of 400 to 500 feet. Ten inches of snow blanketed the runway. But David's dogged determination in simply getting to the airport was something to admire. Birch rocked the wings of the Cub to clean off the snow and loosen the skis and told him he could solo. David took off. "Something quickly came to mind. Birch had told me in my third hour that if I had engine trouble, I should immediately pick out a field on the left or right, BUT DON'T CHANGE (from that choice)! I decided to fake a conked-out engine. I was looking on my left and right for a field I would use. I was gone awhile. Birch stood in silence in the freezing cold on the runway, listening for any sound that could be an engine, wondering where I was, if I was safe. When I finally landed, I got the question 'Why were you gone so long?' We were sitting around the hangar another time, and there sat parachutes that had to be worn when doing spins. I had never really seen them ever used. I didn't know if they had ever been inspected or repacked, or if they were safe at all. But I said to Fuzzy, 'Take me up, and for $20 or flying lessons, I'll jump (using the chute) right NOW." Now that is imprudent enthusiasm. Chuck Dickey let David fly his Cub at his grass field in Slippery Rock, in exchange for some field mowing. One night in '47, David's flight got him back after dark. Chuck was there waiting and turned his car lights on to spot a landing place. Planes can be flown alone, but safer with friends.

Spring of '46 was the start of the busiest and most social time at the airport. Soldiers had returned from war, could use their benefits for lessons and were looking to have some old-fashioned fun. The common interest of flying melded various backgrounds, ages and personalities. These student pilots bonded that spring, some for the rest of their lives.

When you attend school in a one-room classroom for years, you had better get along with people. Ray "Rocky" Filer, a true gentleman, planted seeds for lifelong friendships there and found himself and his passions. Born in 1924, Rocky grew up in Mercer County on a farm not far from the Chadderton farm. He and Earl Chadderton were, and still are, best friends. Older brother Ed began to take flying lessons off Newt Skelton of Mercer. With only three and a half hours of instruction Chadderton bought a new Cub Coupe ('37-'39) that he kept at their farm. Teens Earl and Ray were asked to gas it and "put it away" after Ed's trips. Without specific permission, they would also taxi it around the fields. One day they pulled back the throttle, and had it two feet off the ground. Should they risk and take it higher for a thrill? Or put it back on the ground? Caution prevailed: they put it back on the ground. Ed would have the honor of its first accident.

High school was more than three miles away from home, with no transportation provided. At 15, Ray opted for the practical choice of work and lifelong self-education. He was hired as a painter

Night flights interrupted the movie experience at the Larkfield Drive-In, which is still standing. The rear side was painted white and served as the screen.

at an auto body shop for awhile, and then at 18, entered the Army Artillery. Later he transferred to an Air Force trucking company that transported the men of the 9th troop company into D-Day. By December 1945, he was home from war.

"I was always interested in flying in the worst kind of way," Rocky humbly states. I went out to the airport to talk to them about when they would have VA approval to instruct using the GI Bill benefits (as payment). They weren't sure, so I asked, 'Could we drive down to Pittsburgh and find out?' Bob Hockenberry, Bill Raymer and I drove down to the VA, and they said the Grove City Airport was already approved." With that, Rocky began his formal flying training, soloing on March 18, 1946. "Birch was my teacher, the best instructor at Grove City. Everybody loved your dad.

Whenever a new plane came to the airport, he would say 'What kind of a monstrosity is that?' Rocky got his commercial and instructor's license and did dual instruction on a job basis. "One night, Birch was teaching ground school in the upstairs classroom over the hangar. There was a plane in the shop at the far end of the hangar. Ernie the mechanic was running its annual (check-up) and left a flashlight on — on the airplane's battery underneath the seat. It shorted out, got hot and started a fire. Someone went outside for a smoke, spotted the fire and called the fire department. The fireman wanted to chop a hole in the large hangar door. Birch told them, 'If you want to get in, chop through the small door' (that entered from inside the hangar). When they finally broke in, the fire was almost out, and the plane was no more. But the hangar door was intact.

"Birch had another problem on certain nights. When a student did a night flight and took off on the north runway, the plane would climb right over the screen of the Larkfield Drive-In Theater on Route 58 owned by Bill DeMarsh. Moviegoers couldn't hear their speakers, blew their horns and complained to the manager. The manager would call the police, and a policeman would drive to the airport and complain to Birch."

Rocky became an instructor and taught himself plane-building and restoration. Johnny Neel aptly describes Rocky: "He was the iron man of the whole group — always helping everyone."

I remember the guys' names from this time, though I was a young 3 to 5 years old. But I remember only one in person. I can see his flashing smile and twinkling, devilish eyes to this day. He had a personality as big as life, and lived to the fullest. That was Jack Mars. Bill Raymer observed early, "He had a personality, that even if he said nothing, he would attach himself to you." Everyone can tell

The Birch girls, Jinny, Julie and Jane, loved to visit their dad, Gardner, at the airport.

you stories about Jack Mars!

Jack grew up in the Brent, Pa., area with one younger brother, Bob. His father, John, was an electrician for a coal company. His teen mother, Margaret Hedgland, was one of 18 children and part American Indian. Love of flying came early to Jack. At age 8, he begged his mom to let him take a ride in a barnstormer's plane; both went up together. At Plain Grove High School, he played clarinet and saxophone in the band and graduated in 1942 with one claim to fame — he was 12th out of a class of 13. No doubt Jack took first place for having fun. Robert "Scotty" Scott, the mechanic at the airport from '46 to '49 tells, "After high school, Jack decided to see if he could get into the Air Force. All the work had been done except to be sworn in. His dad was driving him there, when Jack said, 'Dad, turn around. If I have to get up this early each morning, I don't think I want to go.'"

Instead he went into the Army Air Corps, hoping to get pilot training. In less than two months and with only a few hours in the Arkansas air, he was pulled from that post. War has its own needs. There was a shortage of medics in MASH units in Europe. Mars was trained and got his assignment at age 20 — surgical technician with the 90th division of the Third Army. He was shipped to Normandy in August of '44. His new role disparaged theoretical book learning; it was 24-7 of hands-on flesh and blood and body parts. Life and death were a daily schedule in a MASH unit; soldiers witnessed obscene assaults on human bodies. GI Jack was forced in a split-second to observe, evaluate and act — skills he could later use as a commercial pilot.

Gardner Birch instructs Jack Mars in the cockpit of a PT19. It is Birch's favorite photo: 'We were at that moment Van Heflin and Errol Flynn.'

From Normandy, Jack would join the offensive push by George Patton in the Battle of the Bulge. The battle began on December 16, 1944, one of the coldest, snowiest days in memory. Casualties from exposure to extreme cold grew as large as the losses from fighting. The Allies had been able to advance toward the Germans faster than anticipated. The rapid advance, coupled with an initial lack of deep-water ports, presented the Allies with enormous supply problems. Raymer quotes a story from Mars. "Jack was sent out in an ambulance for supplies. While they were gone, the Germans captured the field hospital where the men were being treated. Wounded Germans were brought in. All patients, including the Germans, were treated equal by the doctors and medics. By the time Jack and the supplies returned, the enemy had left: they were pushed back and defeated." The fight that cost 80,987 American casualties officially ended January 15, 1945. Jack was released from duty in February and returned home. He had graduated from class clown to lauded veteran with three battle stars and an award letter from Hap Arnold for valiant efforts to help defeat the Germans.

Just short of his 21st birthday but now more worldly wise, Mars returned to Mercer County and went to work at the Sharon Steel. He earned extra money by playing in local bars and clubs on weekends to support his passion for cars, silk suits and flying. Now with his GI benefits, he could get back to his thwarted dream of becoming a pilot. Birch was now 36, Mars was 22, and at very different points in their lives. But they clicked. Birch, with a good sense of humor, fell prey to Mars' magnetism. Mars adored his

instructor, was a quick learner and soloed under Birch's command on April 29, 1946. In the coming months while working on the airport's service line, Jack earned more difficult licenses and ratings. Although young, he knew when to be serious and when he could have fun.

Jack and Willie Raymer socialized together. Both had been overseas during the war, had matured from their experience and liked the opposite sex. "We loved to go to polka dances at local pubs or beer joints on Friday or Saturday nights. He (Jack) could go and ask any woman — even if they had a husband—to dance, and they would always accept. He was a GOOD dancer. We went to this place where there were always a mother, her 16- to 18-year-old daughter and a third woman. The third woman would always polka with the daughter. One night the third woman wasn't there and Jack danced with the daughter quite a bit. Next time, all three were there. Jack danced with the daughter one time, and the woman came over and hit the roof. She called Jack every name in the book and told him to never dance with the girl again. We figured she must be a lesbian since she had raised so much trouble. Jack also had this little book—about 3 by 2 by 1/4 inches—that he kept in his breast pocket. He had stories written down, funny stories he had heard in his lifetime. If he was ever asked to be an emcee, he was ready with his book. He was a fun guy with off-the-cuff sayings. But not a guy who needed attention."

He continued, "One fall, a group of the guys went deer hunting—Jack, Birch and a friend of his and me," remembers Raymer. "Jack shot a buck and tied it on the roof of his car. We stopped at a

Gardner Birch celebrates a hunting victory.

Jack Mars 'pilots' and Posy Thompson 'props' on a fun day at the airport. Pranks and jokes were common and these two led the way.

beer joint in Clarion on the way home. When we came out, the deer was gone! The law was one deer per season, whether buck or doe. Jack bought a second license so that he could get the tag you had to have to attach to a deer if you shot one. In doe season, we all went hunting again near Kane. We arrived while it was still dark and waited 'till 7 a.m. Jack bagged a doe and put it in his trunk—it was small. Going home, a game warden stopped him, inspected the deer and the second tag, and sent him on his merry way. "

Jack and Posy Thompson were tight airport buddies. Both had survived the grueling European War theater. Back now, and in their early 20s, they valued this new camaraderie and worked hard to make up some of those carefree times they had missed. Posy remembers, "About the photo you have of Jack and me and the toy airplane. Hangar space was scarce and when there was no room at the inn, planes were tied in a row outside. Some happy jokester, we never found out who, brought the toy and tied it down between two real airplanes with a hawser large enough to restrain a battleship. It looked so incongruous that you had to laugh just looking at it."

Even as a teen, Bill Webster had a love for hunting and guns. He graduated from Grove City High School and went to work for Cooper-Bessemer. When WWII began, he enlisted in the Army Air Corp in '42 as an armorer. He was all over Europe and England repairing large guns on Army Air Force military planes. Home in January of '46, he went back to Cooper-Bessemer as a blueprint supervisor. And he took flying lessons that led him to a solo flight on May 1, 1946. Bill had big

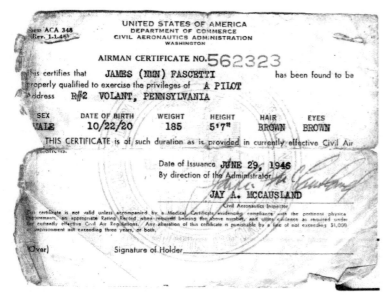

The airman certificate for Jim Fascetti confirmed he was a pilot.

feet that almost caused him to wreck. His size 13 or 14 shoe got caught in a rudder pedal (which turns the plane left or right) on take-off and he was veering toward a stand of trees. He had to immediately push the throttle and increase power to go up and over the danger. Once cruising, he was able to free his shoe. On landing, his instructor confirmed that he had made the correct and only move to save himself and the plane.

James Fascetti was living in Volant when he went into the Army in '41. Once home he took lessons with his GI benefits. His wife, Hilda, remembers him telling her that he "scared the neighbors off the roof they were fixing when he buzzed over their house." Daredevil antics were common among these young, new pilots not thinking of possible danger.

Another local from the Grove City area was Bob Hockenberry, who became a carpenter with the Book Davis Hardware Company. Bob soloed on May 16, 1946, and had several good friends at the airport: Rocky Filer, Gene Rodgers, Bill Raymer. Those friends, flying and the airport were

a major part of his life for many years.

Arthur "Jim" Hepler was born in New Bethlehem, Pa., with a love for music in his bones. At age 7, he started playing the trumpet and played "Taps" in the church steeple. There was no formal training—this was all by ear—but he did learn to read music. He played in high school bands and even played a little when drafted into the Army in '41. Sent to Marseille, France, Jim was in an engineering division and surveyed and built bridges. He came back in '45 with the rank of a Major and joined the reserves. He began at Penn State in industrial engineering while still taking flying lessons at the airport. He soloed in May 1946, and graduated from college in '49.

One of the original CPTP instructors was Clarence Bell from Clintonville, fondly nicknamed "Ding Dong." After the CPTP was cancelled, he chose to enter the Air Force and drew a dangerous assignment: "flying the Hump." The Hump was the name given by Allied pilots to the eastern end of the Himalayan Mountains over which they flew from India to China to resupply the Flying Tigers and the Chinese Government of Chiang Kai-shek. It was considered most important to the successful end of the war in the Pacific. It was a risky endeavor where violent turbulence and terrible weather were standard. Transport planes flew round the clock, some crews doing three round trips a day. Due to the isolated region, parts and supplies to keep planes flying were in short supply, and flight crews were often sent into foothills to gather up debris from previous crashes for parts to repair the remaining units in the squadron. Monthly losses reached 50 percent of

Montgomery Builders had two airplanes: this Navion (with Tommy Harrington on the wing) and later a De Havilland. Clarence Bell was the company's private pilot.

John Krofcheck's log book is a reminder of great memories of flying days gone by.

aircraft flying at the Hump. Clarence came back from his service and was an instructor at the airport for a while. Then in '46, he became a pilot for Montgomery Builders, a large construction firm with a retail lumber yard in Grove City.

Returning home, Clarence came back to the airport and replaced instructor Max Palmer. He occasionally taught John Krofcheck if Birch was busy. John had grown up in Mercer County and dropped out of high school to work, first at Wendell August Forge then in the tool room of Cooper-Bessemer. He signed up as a voluntary draftee and entered the Army, progressing from infantry to M.P. to security. He went in and out of the service several times. His first time out, a number of friends (Rocky, Jack Mars, Bob Hockenberry) were taking flying lessons at the airport, so he signed up too, using his benefits. A story John can't forget happened 60 years ago. "I had to fly another half-hour (in a plane with no lights) to get enough hours for my cross-country. But by the time I got into Mercer, it was quite dark. Mrs. Skelton was signing log books and volunteered to drive me to Grove City. I decided to fly since my girlfriend was waiting for me. Once in the air, it

was pitch dark. There are low power lines by Slippery Rock; I had to light my cigarette lighter to see my altitude. When my girlfriend heard my engine, she turned on the lights of her car to guide me in. The next day I had to take my flight test. Your dad was riding shot with me. My landing was not very smooth, it was very shaky. But Birch said, 'Don't let that bother you, I remember that great landing you did last night.'"

Another instructor at this time was James A. Kennedy. Jim was raised on a farm in Murrinsville, Pa., by unmarried grand aunts and uncles. He graduated from Grove City High School, then from Pennsylvania State University with a degree in agriculture. In March of '43, he entered the Aviation Cadet Program and was shipped a year later after training to Italy, where he flew escort missions as a Second Lieutenant for the 15th Air Force Bombers. He got out in October 1945 and was given a commercial pilot's license. In the spring of '46, having failed at farming, he went to the airport to get his instructor's rating. Birch qualified him in a month, and he taught new students through August of '47, when he decided to become a doctor. The airport connection introduced him to Gordon Lefebvre, and he asked the Cooper-Bessemer CEO to write him a letter of recommendation. After one more year at Penn State for additional classes, he entered the Temple University School of Medicine in September 1947.

Edison "Eddy" Black had been driving a car since he was 11 or 12, so it was normal for him to fly a plane at 14. Eddy grew up on a farm in Grove City and was very independent from the get-go. Maybe it was in his genes. His father, who flew himself in the '20s, was a diesel test engineer at Cooper-Bessemer and a full-time farmer, owning the first combine in Mercer County. His mother was a nurse, handled the business operations of the farm, was very involved in the church, all while raising her kids. Eddy remembers sitting for hours looking at the flight magazines that his dad bought. He scratched together change from odd jobs and paid for plane rides at the airport. Finally his father said, "Don't give him rides, give him lessons!" Eddy would drive out for lessons at age 14, and drive home fast so he didn't get caught. The summer after his 16th birthday he made it happen. "I had been shooting landings, so Birch had me take off and land again and again. Finally he said, 'Did you feel that tire? Let me check it.' He got out, kicked the tire, stuck his head back in, fastened the buckle, shut the door, and said, 'It's all yours.' It was thrilling! The plane jumped off the ground without your dad. I took off and landed a number of times. Reluctantly, Gardner Birch intervened, 'It's getting dark and your depth perception changes at dusk, you need to come in now.'" Eddy soloed on June 15, 1946.

That young flyer had other stories Birch didn't know. "And he would have been mad if he had found out. There was a guy from Brent who was older and a fairly new pilot (Jack Mars, age 22). He'd say, 'Follow me and see if you can keep up.'" Eddy, age 16, was in one Piper Cub, Jack was in the lead in another. They played chase with Wilson Aviation's planes through the strip mines. "Cuts were made in the earth with the dirt piled high on either side. If the cut was wide enough, we could fly down at ground level through the mine areas," Eddy remembers. Trust the author—there would have been hell to pay had Birch found out!

This project allowed me to travel back in time to get to know my father through his friends and their eyes. Bill Raymer said, "I looked up to your dad as a father figure, my own father was killed when I was 11." At 80 years old, he has an unbelievably sharp mind; he remembers everything and has contributed much of the factual information for this book. He is gentle to his core, grateful and content with his life and speaks in a soft folksy style, often ending a sentence with "and so it is." Of all the airport men, Bill reminds me most of Dad—at a very young age, both were thrust into challenges that matured them beyond their years.

Bill was living on the family farm in Grove City when he saw his first barnstormer at the age of 7. It was seeing that old WWI Jenny that had him saying, "I'm going to learn to fly someday." Farm and family life drastically changed when he was 11. His dad and two older sisters were riding in a wagon when it was struck by lightning. The girls and horse were knocked down but his father was instantly killed. His mother, in shock, barely survived until she first hired a farmhand, then later remarried. Bill helped his stepfather make it work. In February of his senior year in '44, he along with 12 others quit school and joined the Navy. They were later awarded their diplomas in absentia.

Bill was a seaman aboard the Navy oil carrier, the USS Cossatot, serving first in the Atlantic and North Africa. The ship came back to dry dock to be retrofitted for the Pacific. He remembers how strange it was to be in Aruba at Christmastime in a tropical environment. Going through the locks of the Panama Canal was fascinating. In Hawaii, the troops received orders to Ulithy in the South Pacific. Bill served until March of '46 and returned to the family farm at age 20. He rode his motorcycle out to the airport, talked to Birch and signed up for lessons.

His solo in July followed the Birch instructor's pattern. "We were shooting landings," Raymer recalls. "'Hold it a minute,' Birch said. 'Something is wrong with the tail wheel.' He got out, checked the wheel, came and buckled the seatbelt and said, 'Go ahead and get out of here.' Another time Birch was checking me out in the PT19. You have to be able to stall, spin, then correct the stall. I wasn't doing it right, more like a tight spiral. Birch showed me how to do it. 'When you want to recover from the spin, push the stick ahead.' Now I did a good spin! I looked back and couldn't see your dad. He never said anything, but I think he blacked out."

Bill began to work as a line boy on Sundays and was given the nickname "Willie." In addition to gassing and moving planes, along with general grunt work, he helped haul people. For $2 per person, the public could fly for 10 minutes in a Piper PA-12 cruiser. "The only time I got upset as a pilot was the time I was hauling passengers. I made three attempts before I could land. Birch then took them up and said he knew what had gone wrong—the wind had shifted. Birch was a teacher and a leader. The new students were taking their ground school classes from someone else. They all flunked their tests. Birch said, 'The hell with this, I'll teach them.' They all passed." Bill got his commercial license and even took a test for United Air Lines. But that was not to be. Bill bought a WACO UPF7 in April '47 and to support his flying habit, he went to work at night for Cooper-Bessemer as a diesel tester. That gave him daytime hours at the airport, for growing friendships and flying.

"No one was too enthusiastic about me flying except me." Una Hart had been married a year and wanted to fly. So she went to the airport and Fuzzy took her up in a trial flight. When she told him she had to throw up, he told her matter of factly to use the window. After that initial flight, Gardner Birch took over as her instructor. "I was practicing emergency landings and I thought he kept yelling, 'Lower, lower, lower!' Then he yelled, 'Higher, higher, higher!' I wasn't afraid though. Maybe that was the type of student I was—I needed more brains. After I soloed on July 13, 1946, I decided to fly over my old home in Stoneboro, Pa. I buzzed the place, and my mother came out screaming, 'Go back, go back, go back!'"

Officially, he is not on any board because his solo at the Grove City Airport was in 1941. Unofficially, his presence at the airport was as strong as any of those listed. Fred Thompson, from Harrisville, came to the airport because, in his words, he had "The Disease" (addicted to aviation). Because his family had a local wholesale floral business, someone nicknamed him "Posy." Even at 85, his technical knowledge of planes of this era and of flying is top-notch, and his writing is a joy to experience. Only his hearing is waning a bit. He worms his way into hearts and his stories are irresistible.

"In a small town in Western Pennsylvania, two local pilots bought an Aeronca C-3. No airport being available, the ship was tied down in a depression in the middle of a field a few blocks from my home. What a bonanza for a 15-year-old boy already afflicted with 'The Disease.' When I was only 5 years old, my father lifted me onto the wing of our local hero Oakley Kelly's bi-plane. That is when I caught the bug—never to recover. Ten years later, 'The Disease' now firmly entrenched, I found a real live airplane parked practically in my backyard! Not one to miss an opportunity, I spent every minute I could, whether in, on or under the plane just in case a flight might be imminent.

"In the meantime I made myself useful. I wiped the dust off, cleaned the windscreen, checked the oil and lugged five-gallon cans of gas out to the ship. I was taught how to prop the plane. Next I was allowed to taxi the plane back out to the swale in mid-field and tie it down, thus saving my idolized pilots the long walk back to the road. It was easy to see how things progressed from there.

"Once I was sure the pilots had departed, I was now the boss. As the weeks passed, the taxi became faster and faster and longer and longer. By fall I was running with the tail up and finally lifted it off—and immediately put it right back

down! I ended up flying a hundred feet or so down the field at a giddy two feet off the ground. I repeated this maneuver for the rest of the summer. When winter came, the owners hangared the C-3 in Youngstown, Ohio, and they never brought it back. So ended my illustrious flying career, at least for three years.

"I got my first real dual instruction at Greenville Airport. The instructor was having marital problems and when it was his turn for custody he brought his 2-year-old son to work with him. We could not leave the child unattended, so he was installed in a canvas sling in the baggage compartment behind the rear seat. The student occupied the rear seat in a J-3 so I had this little rascal breathing down my neck while I was shooting landings (practicing landings). I will say he slept most of the time although I wondered how, as I made some tremendous bounces. The thing I most remember about the kid was he always needed to blow his nose. Hopefully not down the back of my neck.

"I think the most valuable lesson I learned from this man was stall spin prevention. A critique was always held after each session. He had one of those huge foot-thick dictionaries that weighs about 12 pounds on his desk. When your attention strayed, he would slip this tome to the edge of his desk and when he was discussing not turning back to the field if the engine failed on takeoff, he would push if off the desk and it would hit the floor with a tremendous crash. After a long moment to let it sink in, he would say, 'That is how you will hit the ground if you try to turn back.' It really made a lasting impression on me and saved my tender skin a couple of times.

During my 62 years of flying, I had three engine failures on take-off and I am still here, thanks to that big dictionary.

"In '39, I had a summer job paying $12 a week. By freeloading off my parents, I managed to get a half or an hour of dual instruction. Then came my life's greatest disappointment, I could not pass the physical! But I loved flying so much, I just kept right on with the dual. My vision was only 20-70 in the left eye but 20-15 in the right. Vision was never a problem, except legally. I was caught in a vicious circle: I needed flying experience to get a waiver, but I needed a waiver to get flying experience. Finally an instructor, to whom I am eternally grateful, figured a way out of my dilemma, and at long last I could *legally* fly solo.

"Because of my vision problems, I had no illusions about getting into the Air Force. In fact none of the services would take me, and I tried them all! Of course, I was healthy enough for the draft. I spent three plus years as an M.P. in the Army in Africa, Sicily, Italy, France, Panama and Hawaii. I was in George Patton's 7th Army in Sicily and in the 3rd Army in Europe. I would have been in Japan if we hadn't dropped the A-bomb. I was awarded three battle stars. Occasionally I was stationed near an air base and wistfully watched their operations, but never got near enough to touch a flying machine.

"After the war, I took advantage of the GI Bill to finance my flying lessons at the Conneaut Lake Airport. The owner and chief pilot had learned from a great aerobatics instructor, and we got an early introduction to aerobatics. We used a Fairchild PT-19, PT-23 and PT-26, a Stearman PT-17 and checked out in a BT-13. I liked the BT-13 so much that after leaving that school, I bought one. This Consolidated-Vultee BT-13A had only 50 hours on a new Pratt & Whitney engine and a Hamilton Standard propeller. It had been commissioned by the government for war use and had cost them over $50,000, then sold to me as surplus for $520. I brought it to Grove City, since it was closer to home. This is the plane that I let your dad check out commercial students in exchange for gas." This is also the plane that got him in trouble.

"Flying is demanding enough without being handicapped by strong drink. I was guilty only once and even then there were five or six hours between the bottle and throttle. One Saturday night, Scotty (mechanic Robert Scott) and I visited Conneaut Lake Park and its myriad of bars and night clubs. Of course we stayed until closing time, then wended our merry way homeward. I'm sure we couldn't have found our a** with radar. Somehow we managed to stretch a one-hour trip to Mercer into a four-hour trip. After a stop at the Diner to reinforce the inner man, we proceeded to the airport, where Scotty was living upstairs in the hangar. It was getting daylight and there sat the BT-13 just begging someone to fly her. Scotty suggested that we make a dawn patrol to make sure the good Christians were awake and would not miss early services. The BT was one of the noisiest airplanes ever built. We suspected that we were not top line, but rationalized that if we both ran careful cockpit checks, we should be okay. So off we went rejoicing and deciding that Jack Mars needed a pee call. Some of the mining towns in the vicinity had names and others were identified by the number of the mine, as Number 5 mine, etc. Mars lived in a town named Brent about a mile

Elaine Starr, neighbor to the airport, is poised on Posy's BT-13; she is the future Mrs. Jack Mars.

down the road from Number 2 mine. From our lofty perch we could not decide which was which, so we hung a buzz job on both towns. We got a big laugh not being able to tell Brent from Number 2, while I was confronted with landing the beast. I am happy to say I made a greaser (a landing so slick and smooth you couldn't tell when you touched down). 'The Lord takes care of fools and drunks.' We hit the ready room (a hand-me-down phrase from WWII, a room where pilots waited

orders to fly) and collapsed, but not for long. Here comes Mars, mad as a disturbed hornet. In these small towns people knew that Jack was working at the airport, so they KNEW he was the noisemaker and they were burning up the phone lines laying old Jack out in spades. We thought it was a hell of a good joke and something Jack himself would do, and he knew it. After telling us off, he broke down and laughed, grabbed his trumpet, and blew three or four notes which was all he ever played.

Posy Thompson's Clip-Wing Cub that he bought from aerobatic star Caro Bailey was affectionately named 'Droopy.'

"The BT-13 was by now getting long in the tooth, so I traded it for a Clip-Wing Cub. This bird was on the roster of National Air Shows and was the mount of Caro Bailey, one of the top female aerobatic pilots. Her rival, Betty Skelton, got one of the first Pitts Specials and named it 'Little Stinker.' Caro had to have one too, and I got her Clip-Wing. A lot of modifications had been made on it: anything that weighed anything was removed, eight feet was clipped from the wings, it had no brakes, the fuselage shortened. This ship was a FUN machine and we called her 'Droopy.' One day when there was no help around, I attempted to roll old Droopy out of the hangar, and I managed to stick a wing through your dad's office window. I can't remember how much it cost me to replace that big piece of plate glass, but I remember your father was unhappy with me for a while.

"At this same time I had a boxer dog named Mohammed, Moe for short. I got him as a puppy and taught him only Arabic. That worked all right for a while until he fell in with evil companions at the airport and learned English. This animal loved anything with an engine. He liked to fly and I had

Posy Thompson spends some time with one of his best friends, Moe, a boxer who saw as much flying time as some of the cadets and fledgling pilots at the Grove City Airport.

a special harness that, along with the seatbelt, kept him firmly attached to the back seat. One day while practicing aerobatics, I fell out of an inside loop. When a loop is performed properly you are held firmly to the seat by centrifugal force and all is well. But if you stall out inverted on the top, the airplane and everything in it head for Mother Earth: dirt, dust, old pencils, bolts, gum wrappers, etc., all head for the ceiling, and so would the passengers if not securely fastened down. At the beginning of the loop, as the nose of the plane is pulled up, the horizon disappears beneath the nose with nothing to be seen but empty sky. To keep oriented as you start down the backside of the loop, it is necessary to tilt your head back as far as possible to see the earth return to normal. Now we come to the gist of it all—I fell out of the loop and the afore mentioned debris headed for the roof and so did the dog's jowls. As I looked back over my head, I was greeted by the sight of old Moe hanging upside down in his seatbelt with his jowls hanging up to his eyes, which were bulging out in surprise at this new maneuver. The airport afforded him lots of space to run and run he did. He would chase kildeer birds who would fly around in circles about five feet in the air. I often had to bring him in, he would run until his tongue hung out and I thought he would have a heart attack."

Moe lapped up the life of "man's best friend." Bill Raymer rags on Posy. "He lived up the street from the American Legion in Harrisville. His dog got hooked on beer 'cause Posy took him to the Legion. Every day at 10 a.m., especially in the summer, Moe would go down and wait for the manager to open. The manager would give him a cup of beer in a saucer, and he would mosey on home." Posy's mom, a tee-totaler, kept a protective eye on the fly-boys. "You guys were down at the Legion last night, weren't you? The dog didn't get up 'til noon."

Posy gets back at Bill with this story.

"The picture of the bi-plane in the hangar door with your father, Mars, Raymer and me is Willie Raymer's WACO UPF-7. It is a fine aircraft and in great demand today. It was a little squirrelly on the ground and had been provided with a tail wheel lock to help keep it running straight down the runway. It had two tanks to hold fuel on the top wing. You never wanted to fill the tanks full—it would weigh too much. Willie Raymer struck an agreement to sell the WACO to a car dealer who flew a little: he sold the bi-plane and his old car for a new car. Jack Mars was to check this man out in the WACO, but he didn't know about the weight of the full tanks. I arrived when they were trying to

Willie Raymer's WACO UPF-7 bi-plane with, from left, Gardner Birch, Jack Mars, Fred Posy Thompson and Raymer.

start the engine. So I relieved Jack of his propping duty, and finally the engine caught. They were taking off to the south and were still on the ground at the intersection of the east-west runway and Jack prudently throttled back and attempted to turn on to the east runway. Alas, with tail wheel locked and extra weight, he could not turn the aircraft. They ran off the end of the runway, which was being lengthened with piles of old foundry sand. When the WACO hit the sand piles, over it went on its back. I would like to have a movie of my reaction to this emergency. I jumped up and down and didn't do anything. I could not make up my mind whether to jump in the car and hurry to the scene or run for the fire extinguisher first, because I knew gasoline was running all over the place. While I watched, two figures fell out on their heads, a drop of about three feet. Except for a face of black sand, they were none the worse for their adventure. Mars' first words were 'this would never have happened if you hadn't got the engine running.'" The trade had already been finalized and now the car dealer had to deal with his lemon.

"Another emergency was getting lost and finding a spot to land. There were many more grass air fields in those days to land on if lost. No one admitted being lost, but casually asked the dumbest looking person to show you where this airport was located on the map. Forced landings, while not common, occurred with enough frequency to keep you watching for an available field to get down in at all times. All my life this was always in mind: I can get down in that field, and look for another ahead I can reach, or get back to the one I just passed. I recall one forced landing in a farmer's grain field. When an airplane lands, its wheels are at a standstill and slide along until they reach the speed of the airplane; this is what makes the black skid marks you see on modern runways. So it is true with grass. The wheels skid along for 15 or 20 feet, tearing up the surface until the wheels reach speed. I plowed a couple furrows in this field. A young man arrived shortly and I said, 'I hope I did not do too much damage to your wheat field.' He said, 'You didn't hurt the wheat,' and after a pause, 'you're in the oats.' Things were not nearly as regimented at that time. One could fly almost as freely then as we drive today. 'Big Brother' was seldom to be seen; it was just kick the tires and light the fires and away you go. I can remember flying over the Capitol and the White House and one need not fly so high you couldn't see the ground."

Fred "Posy" Thompson, who caught "The Disease" in 1923 and whose words you've been reading since page 116, recently e-mailed, "Jean Beraud Villers writes in 'Notes of a Lost Pilot,' 'One loves aviation, even if, like a female spider, it devours its lovers.' In my declining years, I find myself nearly consumed!"

Solo Board 4

THEODORE F. SHAWLEY	JUL·14·1946
LAWRENCE G. JONES	JUL·18·1946
DONNELY	JUL·27·1946
EVERETT BRANDON	AUG·7·1946
WILLIAM RAU	AUG·14·1946
RALPH W. MARTIN	AUG·15·1946
JOHN GAMMON	AUG·22·1946
EVELYN CRAIG	SEP·14·1946
HARRY STINE	OCT·6·1946
CLARENCE PEARSON	OCT·9·1946
ROBIN SCHULTZ	OCT·14·1946
JOHN WOOD	OCT·16·1946
RICHARD DOUBLE	OCT·22·1946
LEROY MILLER	OCT·27·1946
FLOYD MILLER	OCT·27·1946
ROBERTA BURDETTE	NOV·13·1946
GLENN D. FISHER	APR·22·1947
JOHN B. JACK	APR·29·1947
ROBERT E. GIBSON	MAY·11·1947
EDWARD L. THOMAS	MAY·15·1947
FREDERICK H. LYNN	MAY·23·1947
FRANK COMO	MAY·24·1947
RICHARD O. BAILEY	JUL·9·1947
JAMES A. BAILEY	JUL·9·1947
ELLIS KLINGENSMITH	JUL·9·1947
FREDERICK L. BAILEY	JUL·15·1947
JOHN A. BAILEY	JUL·15·1947

BOARD 4

Transition to peacetime was under way in 1946. U.S. industry was idled by widespread labor strikes and federal government control of railroads. Most wartime price controls were eliminated. Locally at Cooper-Bessemer, there were periodic spurts in sales that raised spirits at times, but the overall pattern was sobering. Lingering reconversion from war industry was being accomplished with considerable strain, and the first postwar year was more difficult than any in recent years. President and CEO Gordon Lefebvre attributed much of the company's plunging sales and earnings to sharp increases in the cost of labor and materials and to decreased shipments due to work stoppages. He reported to the board, "Obsolescence prevails in our factories, despite continuing efforts to squeeze out some expenditures for improvements." Lefebvre's focus was "finding new markets for old products and new products for old markets, rather than moving into fields with which we are not familiar." Whether business was up or down, Gordon flew just the same.

Silently, the Solo Boards tell the airport's story: 1946 was the busiest year and May was the busiest month. The war had been over for seven months, and GI benefits produced government-subsidized students. As manager, Gardner Birch worked Tuesday through Sunday. He had Mondays off and Fuzzy took over that day. A lot of hanky-panky occurred on Mondays, according to Bill Raymer. Fuzzy, though married with a daughter, now had a young girlfriend that he had met while working at Cooper-Bessemer. While Fuzzy was in charge, she would spend the night at the airport. Mechanic Scotty said that Birch was quite disgusted with her moral character. Sorry, Dad, Fuzzy was equally responsible! The '40s were still under the double standard! Scotty tells a tale on Birch. "A neighbor of the airport had a big dog that constantly watered the plants. Birch got a BB gun, and when the dog lifted his leg, he shot him in a very tender part of his anatomy. The dog never came back."

Robert "Scotty" Scott had left high school then graduated from the Pittsburgh Institute of Aeronautics and went into the Army Air Corps in '43, working on military planes. In '46 he leased the shop at the Grove City Airport from Fin Wilson and lived upstairs in a room with a cot. Posy Thompson became a very good friend and praises Scotty's mechanical skills. Scotty at age 84 indirectly confirms, "There was this guy from Sewickley, Pa., who owned a Ryan ST (Sport Trainer). He brought it in for its annual inspection. I could see a string hanging down inside the fuselage. I pulled the back seat out and crawled back to inspect. It was the control cable for the elevators, a 7-by-19 cable (seven bundles of 19 wires each rolled to make a cable). Of the seven, six were worn—rubbing and were shredding. I think I saved his life by catching it."

Posy knew Everett "Chink" Brandon, also from Harrisville, who soloed on August 7, 1946. "He was on the GI Bill. I think he owned a war surplus Aeronca Defender. We called them 'Airknockers.' It was from that ship that the only photo I have of the BT-13 in the air was taken. Chink lived for many years in Grove City as a gunsmith."

The one-stoplight town of Branchton was home for Harry Stine. After graduating from Slippery

'Chink' Brandon poses in his Army Air Force uniform and sits pretty upon his return in 1946.

Rock High School, he attended the Pittsburgh Institute of Aeronautics. While working in Presque Isle, Maine, he was drafted into the Army as an aviation mechanic. After Army service in October of '46, he mastered the entire plane. Mechanics he knew, now he learned the art of flying, too.

Clarence "Sam" Pearson claims he got a private license in less time than anyone else at the airport. The desire started when a high school buddy asked him to fly over the Grove City Cemetery to help scatter a favorite aunt's ashes. After getting his private license, he got a commercial license and became a certified flight instructor. That quick licensing process may have led to Clarence's crash. He landed in a field to pick up a lady friend. The field was too short and a crash occurred on take-off, but without injuries. Birch decided not to report this to the CAA, but instead had Pearson work off the damage by instructing, thus getting needed additional flying time.

Little is know about Robin Schultz, but Dick Double believes she was a student at Grove City College. Johnny Neel was at the airport when Robin was there for a lesson. "Gardner got out of the plane, fastened the belt across the seat so it wouldn't interfere with the rudder pedal, and yelled 'Go—get the hell out of here! Do one or two circles, and if you're shaking too bad, come back and park.'" Sounds like a solo day; if it was, it was October 14, 1946.

As a sickly child, Dick Double sat in his basement where his father had a workshop and built models of airplanes out of balsa wood. He dreamed of one day flying. He built many solid silhouette models with wingspans of six to eight inches, painted solid black for aircraft identification by the

Air Force Cadets stationed at the college. Dick's father couldn't pay for lessons, so as a teen he mowed lawns for 50 cents a yard or did other odd jobs. When he had saved $7, he would walk five miles to the airport and take a lesson with Gardner Birch. "No one would do that now," Dick rightfully comments. "Most of the fellows that learned there had their flying paid by the GI Bill. However, I managed to earn my private, commercial and flight instructor ratings with the help of your father. I only had four to five hours instruction before I soloed."

By then, the Piper Cubs at the airport were in competition with two Aeronca 7ACs for instruction. Dick was 19 and working at an auto body shop. Frugal then, as now, he saved enough to go partner with Birch and buy a year-old Piper PA-12 Super Cruiser in '47 or '48 for $2,400. Birch had requested this plane from Fin Wilson to take passengers up on weekends, earning $2 per person for a 10-minute ride. But Fin had ignored him. It's been said that Fin was always short on cash. Birch would have had to be impressed with young Double's financial responsibility or he would not have partnered with him. The sleek Cub was red and cream, had a 100-horsepower Lycoming engine and an electric starter. Dick tells in his deep gravelly voice, "The aircraft had a six-hour range at about 110 miles per hour. I believe the N number was 98914. It was a three-place machine with the pilot in front and two seats in the back. I bought the gasoline and flew the airplane most of the time. Your dad was a great guy. He would place the airplane in the hangar and did not charge me hangar rent."

Dick continues, "Gardner had a man named Morrison rent an Aeronca 7AC to go to Meadville

Dick Double and an unidentified woman stand with the Piper PA-12 Super Cruiser owned by Double and Gardner Birch. The N98914 was purchased in '47 or '48 and featured a 100-horsepower engine, three seats and a six-hour range of 110 miles per hour.

or Franklin or somewhere. On the way, the weather got dicey, and he put down in a cow pasture and left the plane there. A week later, Jack Mars and I took off in the Super Cub, and Jack landed it in that cow pasture. I flew the Cub home, and Jack brought the red and yellow Aeronca back to home base."

Posy remembers the plane. "This was the first new post-war Piper I had seen. Everyone else was flying cheap war surplus aircraft. He was justifiably proud of the machine and liked to take other pilots for a ride. One day he took me and either Scotty or Jack Mars up. He was in the front, we were in the back. We behaved for a while but after reaching cruise altitude, my buddy leaned forward and I leaned forward. The aircraft, now out of trim, nosed forward, and Double trimmed us for neutral. The trim tab control was a crank between the front and back seat. After a pause we leaned back; we went into a climb attitude. Dick immediately trimmed for neutral. This went on, down then up, for about five minutes. When he figured out what we were doing, he slammed the stick forward and about put our heads through the headliner. There was much merriment between the three of us."

About this time, Birch also bought a two-seater, silver Ryan Primary Trainer 22 (PT22) that he had Scotty restore. He would commute from the Chadderton Airport to Grove City in the plane for a short while, then sold it for a small profit. As fewer GIs signed for lessons, civilian aviation searched for new ways to make money. They approached anyone and everyone with a flying interest. Many salesmen can tell of a time when things slumped, they sold their souls and approached the wrong client and lived to regret it. Birch's most difficult students were at hand. Posy tells the story of the four Miller brothers: Buck, Leroy, Floyd and Milo.

"There was a family with four boys who were fairly hard-nosed—the Miller boys. They had horses and motorcycles and six guns and stuck together like glue. Get in trouble with one and you had three more big boys on your back. They were not outlaws, just born 50 years too late. They decided that their 84-year-old father needed to learn how to ride a motorcycle. They put him on a bike out in the pasture where he couldn't hit anything and he promptly broke his leg. They were jumping a motorcycle out of a second-floor door in the barn into a pile of hay. The bike set the hay on fire and they lost the bike. The oldest Millers decided they wanted to learn to fly, Milo would learn later (Board 5). Birch was the unlucky instructor. Both Leroy and Floyd soloed on the same day (October 27, 1946), and Birch thought his troubles were over. But down country, 15 or 20 miles away, there was a saloon with a beautiful half-mile-long field next to it. One day the oldest Miller landed on this field and visited that bar, then attempted to return to the G.C. Airport. He landed one field short of the airport on the wrong side of the road. He did not crack up the ship but he was running, stumbling drunk. Birch had some harsh words with him, the gist was 'go away and don't come back.' Don't tell I gave their names. The younger ones may still be extant and come after me with their trusty six guns."

Only one more student soloed that fall and the Boards were silent until the spring of 1947. But in the worst of the winter there was a significant happening at the airport. Whispers and gossip around town bring it to light. "Did you hear that Fuzzy DeArment left his wife and daughter for 20-year-old Fern Hagan? The daughter he had promised to teach how to fly when she was 16? Supposedly he told his wife he was going to the Midwest to look for a job. But he took the new car AND the Piper Cub and they BOTH went." Fuzzy was grouchy and went around grumbling and growling like a bear, had a bad temper, kicked and spit and carried on sometimes like a jackass. But once Birch understood his way, Birch could deal with him. Fuzzy was funny and hysterical wanted to be around planes 100 percent of the time. He would do anything that Birch asked him to do. If Birch was doing a nasty, horrible job, Fuzzy worked with him without complaint. But it was the beginning of the end when Fuzzy left.

Robert "Hoot" Gibson was another Harrisville resident and was one of Posy's best friends. "We used to visit the flesh pots of Conneaut Lake Park on weekends. We would fly the BT to Conneaut Lake Airport, hitch a ride down to the lake and take a ferry to the park. One week when I was chasing skirts elsewhere, Hoot decided to go it alone.

Conneaut Lake Airport left something to be desired, like a longer runway. Old Hoot scared himself so bad going into that little airport that he would not fly the airplane home. I had to retrieve it the next weekend."

Another Harrisville teen and third cousin of Posy was Fred Lynn. Fred enlisted as a senior in the Army Air Force in February of '44. And, like Bill Raymer, he was given his high school diploma in absentia. He spent three years as a military pilot in logistics: hauling needed supplies such as parachutes, toilet paper and K-rations all over Europe. Returning in '46, he used his GI benefits to get his civilian pilots license. He went to work for Cooper-Bessemer and was called back into the service twice more—in 1947-48 and during the Korean War. Home again and with a young family, he couldn't afford to keep flying.

During February of '43 in his high school senior year, Ellis Klingensmith was hired at 17 by John Tyndall as a line boy at the airport at the start of the CPTP. He was taught to prop the planes, gas them, take them in and out of the hangar. This hands-on work led Ellis to enlist in the Air Corps in July of '43 after graduation. In tech school, he learned to fix both the plane and its engine. Much as he loved planes, it was clear to him when discharged in March of '46 that the aviation business was going downhill. So, he chose to go to work for Cooper-Bessemer, yet used his GI benefits to take lessons. He remembered his instructor, Birch, from the CPTP. Ellis "followed him through. I mimicked him with the stick and the rudder pedals" and soloed when he was 22 on July 9, 1947. Now he could both fix a plane and fly one.

As much as the four Miller brothers were red-

Hoot Gibson, Betty Pearson and Jack Mars showcase life in the 1940s.

necks, the five Bailey brothers were poster boys for WWII. They bring to mind, but with less tragedy, the story of the Fighting Sullivans. Five sibling Sullivans—George, Frank, Joe, Matt and Al from Waterloo, Iowa —whose motto was "we stick together," enlisted in the Navy on January 3, 1942, with the stipulation that they serve on the same ship. In February, they were assigned to the USS Juneau, a newly commissioned cruiser bound for the Pacific. Even then, the brothers enjoyed the celebrity for being the only five members of a family serving simultaneously in one vessel. Tragically, they all perished when Juneau was sunk by a torpedo during the Battle of Guadalcanal in November 1942. Frank, Joe and Matt died instantly, Al drowned the next day, and George survived for four or five days. As a direct result, the War Department adopted the Sole Survivor Policy, stating that if a family member has been lost as a result of military service, the remaining family members should be protected. The Navy named two destroyers "The Sullivans" to honor the brothers. Their story was filmed as the 1944 movie "The

Fighting Sullivans," and inspired, in part, the 1998 film "Saving Private Ryan."

The story of the Bailey Brothers—Fonnie, John, Dick, Fred and Jim —began in the early part of the 20th century in Harrisville on the 75-acre farm of grandparents John and Hannah Bailey. Unable to have children, they adopted a son, Otis. Hannah's brother and his family, who lived next door, did not accept the adoption. In retrospect, Fonnie believes that his grandmother's brother wanted the valuable 75-acre farm to remain with blood relatives. In the '20s, Otis and his wife, Frances, began a family. A trouble shooter at Cooper-Bessemer, Otis was sent to Oklahoma to repair some large diesel engines. When it was apparent that this job was not short-term, Otis came home to get his family. John and Hannah pressed to have Fonnie, the oldest at age 6, stay at the farm with them. His parents relented, took the rest of their children and stayed in Oklahoma for about 10 years. Fonnie was put to work with farm chores and never saw his family until around 1936. Even when his family returned, Fonnie continued living with his grandparents, working on the farm and at the Bowie Coal Company. John died in 1940. Fonnie joined the Army in 1944 and became a truck driver in infantry transportation. Shortly after he enlisted, the farm was sold and Hannah was committed to Warren Mental Hospital. A nurse told Fonnie, "Your grandmother should not be here." Otis eventually got a bill from Warren for her care. A lawyer he consulted asked, "Did you have her committed?" Otis said no. "If you didn't put her in, you don't owe the money." When Hannah died in '53, Otis and Fonnie paid for her funeral. After his Army duty, Fonnie went back to Bowie Coal as a truck driver. Though

his brothers took flying lessons when they returned, Fonnie's work ethic kept him from asking for time off to join them for a little fun.

Dick is the first brother listed on the solo boards, though he was the third Bailey son. He went into the 13th Air Force, 344 service squadron, at age 19 and spent five years in the jungle islands of the Pacific fixing aircraft. The youngest and fifth Bailey, Jim, had the toughest time getting into the service. He had to get past his parents, who already had four sons in active duty and were very aware of the risks. He went to enlist in the Navy, but because he was a young 17, had to have his parent's permission. Otis refused to sign, as did Frances. For two weeks, Jim followed his mom around wherever she went with the permission paper in his hands. Children are masters at this; he wore her down and she signed the paper. While aboard the USS Helena headed for Europe, the U.S. declared victory. Jim was devastated; he now felt he hadn't done his part. He would persevere in proving his allegiance by being involved in three world wars. Brother No. 4, Fred, joined the Army and was in a tank battalion under Patton in Europe. He got shot in the stomach in Germany and was a prisoner of war there. This injury doomed his future health. John, the second son, was a radio operator in the Army's Signal Corps in Europe. He was knifed while in bed in Africa, but recovered. All five brothers, unlike the Sullivans, returned from war alive. Buried under their usual quietness was a need for adventure, a sporadic impulse to live on the edge. The four who were raised together celebrated by signing for flying lessons. Those Baileys (Dick, Jim, Fred, John) soloed within a week of each other in July of 1947.

The Bailey Brothers during World War II: Fred (Army), Fonnie (Army), Jim (Navy), John (Army) and Dick (Air Force).

Posy remembers these brothers, too. "Dick and his brother, John, were learning to fly at Grove City. Dick had advanced to the Fairchild PT-19. The Bailey homestead was about 10 miles east of the airport. The home sported a nice, big pine tree in the front yard. One day, Dick came back to the airport with the top of that tree caught in the tail wheel. It was very hard to explain this to Mr. Birch. Back in those days the government frowned on parachute jumps. There was all kinds of paper work involved if one wanted to go brolly-hopping. The Bailey Brothers were not much impressed by regulations. One day, over the airport, comes an airplane piloted by Dick, and John comes floating gently down in a borrowed jump sack. Things were more fun in those days."

Joyce Bailey, Jim Bailey's only daughter, recounts. "Rules are necessary for order, particularly in the work environment. But the Bailey family doesn't like restraints put on them. In their free time, they want to do what they want to do! John was the character in the family, the most raucous. One day he flew under the Emlenton Bridge. A man in a boat was convinced he was about to be hit and jumped from the boat, which then drifted downstream. At a later time at his mother's funeral, a stranger came up to John and said, "You're the S.O.B! I'm the guy in the boat you almost hit!"

Solo Board 5

MILO L. MILLER	MAY·20·1947
EDWIN W. FITZGERALD	JUN·11·1947
EDWARD L. DiCOLA	JUL·16·1947
HENRY R. ZEDRECK	AUG·16·1947
SALVATORE F. PISCIOTTO	SEP·17·1947
JOHN H. ANDERSON	OCT·16·1947
GEORGE Z. BOBO	OCT·26·1947
JOHN R. MORRISON	NOV·9·1947
JUNIOR T. ROBSON	DEC·13·1947
ROBERT S. BLACK	MAY·12·1948
RALPH D. DOUBLE	MAY·16·1948
EDWARD G. McCARL	MAY·22·1948
CALVIN R. FEATHER	MAY·28·1948
JOSEPH F. LUND	MAY·31·1948
DANIEL F. McDEAVITT	JUN·20·1948
JACK F. McNUTT	JUN·27·1948
ALBERT W. McDEAVITT	JUL·5·1948
GEORGE R. BOBO	JUL·7·1948
VIRGIL L. HOVIS	JUL·17·1948

BOARD 5

The first two names on Board 5 are out of chronological order: Milo Miller, one of the infamous Miller Brothers, and Ed Fitzgerald. Ed had been interested in flying all his life. He took two tests to get into the Air Force, but because he had asthma, they wouldn't take him, but the Army did. When he returned, he took flying lessons at the airport. Mostly, his instructor was James Kennedy. But Birch supervised. Ed remembers a dual lesson, "He said 'Cut the throttle and land it.' I looked ahead: there wasn't anyplace. Your dad took control, flew back around to a field we had just passed and pointed that I could land there." Ed had just experienced the important lesson of always having an emergency landing place in your site. Though afraid he would flunk his solo, it didn't happen and he flew alone on June 11, 1947. As part of private license requirements he did his cross-county flight from Grove City to New Castle to Wooster, Ohio. That flight got him his private license. His wife, however, was deathly afraid of flying and, consequently, Ed let his license expire.

Dr. Edward Dicola was an intern at Bashline Rossman Osteopathic Hospital and Clinic in Grove City and so was Dr. Salvatore "Sal" Pisciotto. Both took flying lessons in the summer of '47. Marie Pisciotto remembers, "Sal was born in Brooklyn, N.Y., and interned for a year at Bashline. It was an excellent internship. The town was very different from New York, very residential. We lived in an apartment and socialized with the Italian people in Grove City. We spoke Italian, and there was no Italian doctor in the town. Everyone wanted us to stay and set up a practice. On Sundays all you could do was to go to church and then go home. Sal loved to fly and wanted the lessons, but I was concerned about his safety and didn't want that. I got pregnant and decided to go back to New York to have the baby. I left in August. Sal immediately went out to the airport and took lessons." In November, Sal returned to the Big Apple: a new father, a new pilot, a new family practice doctor.

Henry Zedreck was born in the Slippery Rock area in '24 with a natural ability to fix anything mechanical. He was drafted into the Navy and sent to Texas to fix airplanes. That kept him from being sent overseas. He returned home in '45 and with his passion for aircraft, he took lessons in

'47 and loved it. He flew until he married in '49.

George Bobo was born of humble origins in Kentucky in 1910, and his father died when he was 6. That would have spelled defeat for most kids. But not for George; nothing was impossible to him. He grew up tall, good-looking, a force to be reckoned with. He jumped center on the Caneyville High basketball team the year it won the Kentucky state championship. After school, he went to work for the state highway department, operating a shovel. In 1931 at 21, he went into highway construction for himself. And like many business owners during the Depression, he went broke. Times were tough, and there was no work. In '36 he loaded up his wife and two sons and headed north before the finance company could take his car back.

Bobo arrived in the Darlington/Beaver Falls area of Pennsylvania where he met Albert Bango. He talked Albert into selling his hotel to raise cash and then going into the strip mining business with him. According to his son, Philip, "He could talk the skin off a rattlesnake." Bobo, Bango and Marshall was thus formed.

Ray Bowie, himself a coal company owner and the future father-in-law of Philip Bobo, writes in the Mine History of Mercer County, "George came to Mercer County in '37 with a lot of talent. He was very clever, and work was scarce, and George needed a job badly. Finally one owner said, 'Let's see how you handle a drag bucket.' The mine owner took a silver dollar from his pocket and threw it on the ground and said, 'If you can set the center of that bucket over the silver dollar, you have a job.' George did it. Restless, and not satisfied to just work for wages,

it was not long before he persuaded machinery companies to give him machinery for his business. Starting in Jackson Center, he produced coal, bought more machinery to produce more coal, to buy more machinery.

"WWII was now on with all its restrictions and priorities," continued Bowie. "Those were two words George didn't know. The nation needed coal, and George could get it, if he had machinery. So, Mr. Bobo leased coal lands without coal, then persuaded the government to give him machinery on the strength of these coalless leases. If the heat got too hot, George would sell a $75,000 shovel with one of these leases to another operator for $90,000. He got around these price fixing boys in Washington by saying, 'I sold the shovel for $40,000 and the lease for $50,000,' which was permissible. What the government didn't know was there was no coal on the leases. The purpose of this complicated deal was to sell the shovel to a new owner who did have coal in another district and at a price with a very good profit. It took men like George with drive and determination to win this war. God knows the government inspectors would never have won any war."

George headquartered his business in Grove City after '37 and eventually sold out or bought out other partners until the George Bobo Company was owned solely by him. Bowie continued, "He expanded his holdings at a fantastic rate and so did his spending. He bought shovels, properties and buildings at a furious rate. He bought the property at the corner of Center and Mill Streets and completely remodeled the cellar that had been a livery stable into an elegant playroom. Nothing was spared. But the erstwhile 'Diamond Jim Brady' had another side. When a competitor died, he flew to Saskatchewan, Canada, to bring back a grandchild of the deceased, who would not have gotten home otherwise." If a foreman under him showed promise, Bobo formed a separate company giving him financial backing and putting him completely in charge. He operated a mine in his hometown of Williamsburg, Ky., and owned a Chrysler and Plymouth dealership in Grove City. Now the quintessential self-made man, he had arrived by anyone's standards and his generosity was legendary.

His company already owned two airplanes for its travel that were kept at the Grove City Airport: a single-engine early-model Beechcraft Bonanza with a butterfly tail named "Baby" and a twin-engine Beech D-18 called "Kitten." The twin Beech was a beautiful plane, akin to a Lear Jet. It was king of the hill and very out of place at the grass airstrip with no lighting that it called home. Its pilot was Paul Johnson, a pilot's pilot who had previously worked for the airlines. Bill Raymer praises, "He was so skilled, he could get in and out of the unlit airport at night as nimbly as a J-3 Cub."

The ribbon cutting of the 18th hole at the Grove City Country Club recognized George Bobo, second from left with scissors, who paid for the 18th green. Club pro Neil McHugh is to his right, and next to McHugh is Charles Montgomery of Montgomery Builders and Supply.

According to cool Posy Thompson, 'in my riotous youth' George Bobo's Beechcraft Bonanza 'Baby' with a butterfly tail was a treat to fly.

Posy continues, "George Bobo was universally liked by the airport gang, and no wonder; he was generous to a fault. I don't know how he treated his other employees, but there wasn't anything too good for his pilots. If he bought good quality clothing for himself, he did the same for his pilots. When they flew to New York, George stayed at the best hotels, as did his pilots. They visited the best restaurants and nightclubs and George picked up the check. One time George bought a Chrysler Town and Country Convertible. These were 'Woodies' and were top of the line, and he bought his pilot one, too. Bob Scott, the mechanic, installed a bar in the twin Beech. Occasionally some of the airport hangers-on who knew where the key was were wont to have a 'wee nip' on George. We had been taught

that it was not a crime to steal booze."

There was still one goal to be conquered by George—to learn how to fly his own plane. Birch, his same age, became his instructor. No doubt that with his maturity and drive, Bobo was an eager student. He soloed on October 26, 1947, and in typical big-hearted fashion, he rewarded Gardner with two new, very expensive Hickey Freeman suits. He was now interlaced at many levels to the airport. Scotty adds, "George was a wild spender. He'd fly to St. Louis to get spare ribs if he felt like it. One winter George was flying with his wife, Berta; the runway was snowy and the nose gear collapsed. Neither one was hurt; it wasn't his fault. I never liked the Bonanza—the nose gear was too frail." The mechanic in Scotty foresaw something ominous about that plane. George's oldest son Bob (George Robert Bobo) would solo as a teen the following summer.

Ralph Double was Dick Double's father who worked at Cooper-Bessemer. After encouraging and supporting his son's passion for planes for years, he followed suit after his son and took lessons himself. According to Dick, "After Dad soloed in May of '48, he did go out and do some flying." It's a compliment to their relationship that Ralph could be the follower and accept that he might learn something from the younger generation.

Late in high school, Ed McCarl began several part-time jobs. He started at Wendell August Forge, then a local machine shop. At age 17 or 18, he had scraped enough money for some flying lessons. "The day I soloed (May 22, 1948), I was scared to death. I had wondered if it was going to happen a number of times before. I was pretty tight! I would have liked to stay with it forever, but it wasn't meant to be." The prohibitive cost of flying would prevent Ed from following his heart. In July, he went into the Naval Air Corp and the Korean War for four years. His eyes weren't good enough to pilot, and he ended up flying off the aircraft carrier as a gunner.

Born in Grove City in 1925, Calvin Feather finished high school in Sandy Lake in '41 and went to work for George Bobo until he enlisted in the Army Air Corps in August of '43. He was part of the aviation engineering unit that built airfields in India, Burma and China. Calvin got out in early '46 and rejoined the Bobo Coal Company. Having been around pilots and planes in the service, he could use those GI benefits and learn

to fly himself. Calvin remembers, "Birch was a good instructor. Sometimes he got a little loud when things got as they shouldn't have. I was taking dual and it was pretty windy. I was taking off to the north over the drive-in. There was a strong crosswind. Birch yelled at me to put the wings down into the wind and get the plane straightened up. He told me what to do, as he should have, it was learning lesson. When I did solo, it went well, there was no problem. We all had a great time at the airport." Calvin got his private license and did fly some; again, money limited that occasional yearning.

The McDeavitt grain and cattle farm was in West Liberty and was typical of family life in Western Pennsylvania in the 1920s. Each family member contributed in multiple ways. At an early age, Al and his younger brother Daniel, or "Buck," helped with farming chores. In their teens, they joined their dad in his day job as a block and bricklayer. In '44, Buck was drafted into the Navy. After eight months in South Carolina, he volunteered for sea duty on a cargo ship, just to get to travel. One tour in the Pacific had him delivering three holds full of beer to Manila. He got home in '46 and just wanted to learn how to fly. With a smile on his face and twinkle in his eye, Buck drawls, "I should have been kicked out of the air for fooling around. I flew for about eight to 10 hours after I soloed, but I had bought a new Ford convertible. It was the best car I ever owned and I couldn't afford both." Al soloed a few weeks after Buck in June of '48. With a wife and four children, Al definitely couldn't afford the luxury of flying.

Jack McNutt came to the Grove City area as a

teen with his family. His father was a jack-of-all-trades, but tired quickly of any one job. When Jack was a high school junior, his father left the family. Jack decided not to continue school, but work to help his mother make ends meet. When he was drafted in November of '44, he was working for the George Howe Company, which guaranteed jobs after military service. The Army gave him training for the infantry and then shipped him out for an invasion on Okinawa. While on that ship, it was announced that the U.S. had dropped an atomic bomb on Japan. "Otherwise," Jack states, "I'd have been a foot soldier invading Japan, and no telling how many of us would have been killed on both sides." He completed his duty at a desk job in the South Pacific and returned home in early '46. He went back to Howe, but the personnel manager told him they couldn't take him on. He didn't understand, but accepted it. In time, Pete Beech, Howe's son-in-law, would ask why he didn't return after the war. Pete investigated and found that the personnel manager had judged "guilt by association." Jack had told two acquaintances to go to Howe's for a job. One of them was caught stealing. Pete apologized and immediately offered him a job. He declined. Jack married in late '47 and his first son was born the next spring. He worked two stints in the Cooper-Bessemer Foundry, and he drove trucks and busses. But mainly he would have loved to become a commercial pilot.

Jack began flying lessons as an ex-GI in the summer of '48. Rocky Filer was his instructor for his private license. He worked toward his commercial license under Jack Mars when govern-ment news hit like a bomb—a GI could no longer use his rights to pay for flying lessons. The bill was intended to train men for commercial flight. Too many had used it only for pleasure. Birch wrote letters on McNutt's behalf, but to no avail. Aviation's door was shutting for both of them.

Gardner Birch was a realist. Until then, he had been able to defend the work he loved because it had provided adequate income, along with many intangible rewards. But the government's new policy would change all that. Major cash flow into the airport from GI funding stopped. Fuzzy's day-to-day support was gone, Fin Wilson had no money to provide for basics, and Birch was getting more pressure from his wife, Grace. She wanted him home.

Grace and Gardner were very different in personality and outlook. Grace's issues were deep and she suffered from depression. She was not innately social, confident or happy. Fearful, she had a subtle but powerful way of manipulating, based on logic, fact and reason. For years she reminded Gardner with regularity of the danger of his work. That was a fact. He worked many hours each week. Also a fact. She could not accept and support that he loved managing the airport, flying and his close camaraderie with that gang. She wanted him out of the airport crowd and home with her. Then she would have more of him to herself and she would be happy, too. Fuzzy had been a particular threat to her. She couldn't forget that he had left his family and ran off with a younger woman. Gardner's temptress was the airport and flying. With more logic and fact, Grace could change his mind. The government provided the ammunition when the airport could no longer support the family. Gardner needed to come back to the Hickory-Sharon area and take a secure job with the brick-layer's union. It would be safe, offer more time with the family and provide the money they needed for the future. It all made sense; it was the responsible thing to do. A long time ago, Gardner had committed to marriage and his family; his values were as solid as his stocky body. Now his decision reaffirmed that, but at quite an expense to himself.

In the summer of '48, Jack Mars wrote in his logbook that he had taken over Birch Aviation (at the age of 24). As a single person living at home, Jack might be able to eke out a living as manager of the airport. Bill Raymer reflects on that portentous event. "Anybody that hung around or loafed at the airport believed that (that it was Birch Aviation, but the true ownership was Wilson Aviation). They never thought of Fin Wilson as the person in charge. Gardner Birch was kingpin at the airport. Gardner Birch WAS the Grove City Airport."

His boards hang today as a reminder of a special time and place when those men and women flew proud.

Board 1

Very little is known of 1st Lt. Francis T. Stephens except that he was transferred in the summer of '44 to Lubbock Air Force Base, Texas. On the back of his photo, Fuzzy wrote, "Francis T. Stephens c/o Harry L. Yost, Postmaster, Boise, Idaho. Goodbye, Boy."

Gene Rodgers worked and retired from Cooper-Bessemer. Flying was always a big part of his life. He had more than 50 years of flying experience and ownership in a number of planes. His last was a sharp red, white and blue '47 Cessna 150 with a Continental 100-horsepower engine. He was an active member of Experimental Aircraft Association Chapter #161 in Grove City. Gene's sense of humor contributed to many enjoyable sessions of hangar flying. When Gene got that impish grin, someone was going to get the needle. Gene passed away on March 24, 1994.

Bob McGowan, a very young and active 80, still owns his own real estate company in Slippery Rock. Over his adult life, he started 14 companies, was a commercial developer, built more than 1,000 houses and owned a lumberyard. In addition, he got a commercial pilot's license, was instrument-rated and owned several planes, the last being an Aztec that he had until '83.

Harold Brydon went into partnership with Howard Muse of Pittsburgh and formed the Pilgrim Coal Company. While building a ramp, he had his first heart attack. At Mt. Sinai Hospital in Cleveland, Ohio, he was one of the first people in the country to have open-heart surgery. He never truly recovered and lived in pain until he died in 1958.

Hillis Kemp got out of the Navy in 1946 and went to Ohio State University, getting his teaching credentials. He taught industrial arts in Belmont, Ohio, for 40 years, and he still lives there.

Ray Cornelius came back from the service and went to Grove City College, majoring in chemical engineering. He went to work for Armstrong Cork in Lancaster, Pa. In 1979, he moved back home to Grove City, buying 50 acres with a pond (created after being strip-mined) that he regularly uses for fishing. He and his wife, Jane, also volunteer their time at the Grove City Area Historical Society.

Cooper-Bessemer gained momentum from the nation's economic upswing in 1948 as an engine builder. Industry and business had won the battle for removal of rationing and price controls, which were restraining production and creating stifling shortages of raw materials. Production leapt 18 percent nationwide. President Truman, in an economic report to the nation, characterized construction as being below needs and expectations. In other words, the long-heralded post-war depression doesn't show up in the '48 calendar. The work force was at near full employment.

Cooper-Bessemer's five-year plan of recovery from the debts of 1946 was progressing ahead of schedule. Sales were up and dividends to stockholders resumed. America's business cooled slightly in '49, but Cooper-Bessemer's momentum carried it through the temporary recession. At mid-century 1950, the company was able to report that the major share of profits came from the sale of products developed since the end of WWII. With the 1950 Communist invasion of South Korea, the United States became entangled in another war, which in turn boosted industrial production.

In 1951, Cooper-Bessemer sales of $52,310,978 for the first time surpassed the wartime peak for 1943. Net profits were more than double the '43 figure, and book value, representing common stockholder's capital, had more than tripled. Additional land was purchased in Grove City, and the expansion of buildings, installations and new tooling followed—all good news for Gordon Lefebvre. On the downside, troubles plagued the GMV turboflow engines, and General Electric had come up with a competing package that could revolutionize natural gas pipeline transmission. Cooper-Bessemer was very dependent on a relatively narrow line of products and there was a large age gap between top and middle management, with no plan for succession of leadership. Except for Gordon, all corporate officers had been with the company since the 1930s.

Still, the bottom line in '51 reflected the best year in the company's history, and the levels continued in '52. Gordon could do whatever he wanted, and so he did. He wanted control of the airport, and in '52 he leased it for Cooper-Bessemer

from Fin Wilson. He would use it for his corporate airplanes, for company storage and for personal philandering. First off, he made the executive decision to pave the runways. According to Martin Haski of Haski Aviation in New Castle, "In today's terms, that was probably a $2,000,000-plus decision." George Bobo apparently assisted with the paving, if only with his large earth-moving equipment. Both men loved flying, their planes and the best lifestyles. Gordon used some of the hangar for company storage, and in addition, used the small bedroom above the office as his personal "affair boudoir." Its former inhabitant, Scotty, had never been so lucky.

Posy remembers these events as the end of the airport gang as they knew it. "Gordon could be a crotchety old fart. He decided to evict all privately owned aircraft. It left me with no place to go, so I moved my Clip-Wing Cub over into the shop at the end of the hangar, as far away from the office as possible. I thought I could hide my ship there until I found hangar space. A fast-talking operator from Franklin said he had a buyer and needed to demonstrate it. He returned it one day while I was at work and called my dad and said someone should put it in the hangar. My father, not knowing that I was *persona non grata*, shoved it into the hangar in front of His Highness Gordon Lefebvre's airplane. This enraged the great man and I was informed to remove my plane, post haste. Even old George Monroe, who had worked at Cooper-Bessemer forever, had to move his plane. George took his ancient Aeronca Chief home and flew it from a field next to his house. A number of the other guys went down to Chuck Dickey's field in Slippery Rock. I was so mad about the whole incident, I sold my ship and quit flying for a few years. "

Gordon should have watched his karma. What goes around comes around. The year 1953 was stable. But attempting to pinpoint the cause of Cooper-Bessemer's business disaster of 1954 was like throwing darts at a target with no bull's-eye. There was a nationwide recession, and a strike at the Grove City plant shut down operations for seven weeks in the only production area that had been doing well. And then there was the U.S. Supreme Court decision against Phillips Petroleum and some 8,000 other producers bringing price controls to producers selling gas to interstate pipelines. Construction efforts halted. For Cooper-Bessemer, the accumulation of unfortunate circumstances added up to a 38 percent decrease in net sales and the first net loss since the Depression year of 1938.

Cooper-Bessemer stock dropped to a level far below its book value. Recognizing the company's vulnerability, a wealthy New York investor, Robert New, was quietly putting together a substantial block of its stock. Early in 1955, New made his move to corral a majority interest and take over control of the company. In the midst of the crisis, unforeseen circumstances brought about the resignation of Gordon Lefebvre. While no exact details of Gordon's resignation have been available, Lawrence Williams was summoned by the board of directors to return as president. The board reacted fast and in unison and avoided the attempted takeover. Williams states, "It was a pretty close call, but it actually was a very beneficial experience because it prompted us to turn the company around."

Gordon Lefebvre, West Point adventuresome air-balloon cadet and summersault-shot guzzling Cooper-Bessemer CEO and pilot, at approximate age 65, abruptly left the company and Grove City and went to work for competitor Dresser Clark (now Dresser-Rand) in Olean, N.Y. It is reported that he died while living there.

In the 1960s, Cooper-Bessemer began to diversify, eventually broadening its product lines to include petroleum and industrial equipment, electrical products, electrical power equipment, automotive products, tools and hardware. The CEO was Eugene Miller and with its first name change since the merger of Cooper and Bessemer, the company officially became Cooper Industries (CBE on the New York Stock Exchange) on December 10, 1965. Robert Cizik succeeded Miller in 1975. Bill Raymer, a lifelong Cooper-Bessemer employee, remembers, "We never called it Cooper-Bessemer. To the guys in Grove City it was always Bessemer. Cizik was the last CEO there (while Cooper-Bessemer was in Grove City). He bought up a lot of smaller independent companies. The stock went up and then split. The company was doing great. Cizik was making over $8,000,000. Then he started spinning off companies. He retired and took a wagonload of money, he was one of those crooks." At that time Cooper-Bessemer was under Cooper Cameron (CAM also in Houston) which was spun off in 1995. CAM closed the gigantic Grove City plant. Attempts are being made to lease the vacant space. In 2005, Cooper Cameron became simply Cameron and still provides aftermarket parts for the Cooper-

Bertha 'Birdy' Mueller Heatley reminisces in front of her Board in August 2005.

Bessemer trademark products. Rolls-Royce acquired Cooper-Bessemer in 1999 and took over the local facility in Mt. Vernon, Ohio. Ironically, Cooper-Bessemer's rival General Electric still has a large diesel engine plant in Grove City.

Bertha "Birdy" Mueller transferred to Syracuse University for a bachelor of science degree in commerce. She flew twice out of Cicero, N.Y. Back to visit Grove City in the summer of '46, Dr. Russ Danner and Brenton Holter both took her for a ride. Her last logbook entry was May, 14, 1947. She married engineer Bob Heatley and they lived near Pittsburgh. Birch and Grace visited them there in 1959. Later Birdy moved to California. She stays youthful and energetic by swimming in her pool and working part time for a professor. She and fellow pilots Eleanor Williamson and Dick Double are now friends because of this project and often get together at the Riverside Airport, which is near Birdy. They are a very active California "Solo Boards" contingent!

Evelyn Kreidle got her teaching degree in business from Grove City College. She first taught in New York. Getting a ride to an airport was so complicated that she rarely flew. She later worked in Ohio, where she taught typing, short hand and accounting. When she retired in 1984, she moved back to Grove City. Her typing skills are still very sharp; Evelyn, like many of her fellow pilots, e-mails on a regular basis.

Eleanor Williamson graduated from Grove City College in '46 in business and teaching. The next year she married and moved to California, picturing her future as a modern corporate secretary. Then life happened. A divorce in 1970 sent her back to college to update her teaching credentials. She taught until 1986 then did some traveling. Still in sunny California, she and Birdy have become good friends. They swim for exercise and hang out for fun. Eleanor recently took a sentimental ride in Dick Double's plane.

John Thompson, like Calvin Feather, ran a huge dragline for Bobo Stripping while it was in business. Then he went to work for Cooper-Bessemer, operating different heavy-duty equipment, until retiring in '88. He died in October of 2004 with his wife Dorothy still very much in love with him. Now that was a life well lived.

Board 2

Dr. George Hoover ended up in family practice in Oberlin, Ohio. He practiced for 45 years until 1987. Although his wife was against his flying because of safety issues, he flew until 1980. In addition, he was a Federal Aviation Administra-tion controller physician, giving physicals for the FAA.

Chuck Dickey began his working career for Cooper-Bessemer. After five years, he went into the trucking business, driving at the local level. But he will be most remembered, according to Bob McGowan, "As the man who did more for local flying than anyone. After Cooper-Bessemer leased the Grove City Airport, Chuck opened his farm, licensed as 'Flying Acres,' to his pilot friends who had to move their planes. No rent was ever charged, all he asked was for someone to help him mow on occasion." Chuck owned a Cub, then a Cessna 175. Though it's been 10 years since he flew, he still belongs to EAA Chapter #161. Chuck, a big man with a hearty chuckle, has been success-fully battling multiple myeloma for a couple years.

John Creighton got out of the Marines and went to Penn State University. He graduated in '50 with an agriculture degree and went to work for Penn State as a county agent. For a long time, he had a small farm in Mechanicsburg where he grew peaches, blueberries and other fruits and vegetables. Though now living in a retirement community, he runs a community garden pro-gram and has several colonies of bees.

Johnny Neel plugged away at getting all of his certifications. He hired himself out as a local pilot and flew for George Bobo for a while. Then in 1954, he was taken on as an Eastern Airlines pilot and based out of Atlanta. Neel says, "I was flying a Boeing 727 at LaGuardia Airport when I pulled up behind a plane with a pickle on it. I recognized that Heinz pickle. We picked up the phone and asked them if Jack Mars had retired or was still flying for them." (Jack Mars eventually went to work for Heinz as a pilot; see page 147.) Neel was with Eastern for 30 years and flew his Bonanza back to Grove City around 1995 for a last visit. Johnny reflects on his initial training there, "Everybody loved Gardner, he was a prince." Neel died suddenly from cancer in July of 2006.

Muriel "Dottie" Nelson was already married when she soloed. She didn't fly much after that. Her father-in-law had a greenhouse in Mercer and she and her husband, Harold, worked there. Dottie was a florist until her children were born. In 1980, they moved to Sebring, Fla. In her 80s, she has a keen memory of people and places related to the airport.

Dr. Don Briner continued to practice in Mercer until '54. His wife doctored for two years until her first child was born. In '54 they moved to Detroit and he took a residency in internal medicine. He then practiced in Dayton, Ohio, from 1956-79. The Briners then moved to East Lansing, Mich., where Don became a department chairman at Michigan State's College of Osteopathic School. Betty tells me, "He was a very smart man. I had had a great fear of flying, and he finally got me to fly (com-mercially) when I was in my 40s. We retired (in Michigan), and Don passed away in 1994."

Edith Kinder flew off-and-on during college, then she married Zane Hoffman and raised a fam-

Civil Air Patrol cadets met at Chadderton Airport, circa 1950. The planes, from left, are two Cessnas, likely 170s, and a 195 Cessna.

Ed Chadderton, in hat, and his pilot, Joe Buckwalter, pose with awards they won at the Reading Air Show with Chadderton's 310 Cessna that he kept in a special heated hangar, circa 1950.

ily. Around age 50, she went to work at Victory Elementary School near Barkeyville. She was there for 18 years, ending up as their secretary. Retired, she now lives in Harrisville on a farm that has been in Zane's family for over 110 years.

Ed Chadderton continued to lease the Chadderton Airport from Fin Wilson until 1963 when he purchased it for $40,000. Remember, Ed had made all the improvements with his own money. In 1980, Ed sold the property to FIC, a development company out of King of Prussia; Jack Dulati was a principal. A correction of that deed was made in 1984, with a purchase price of $135,000. Ed Chadderton, a true entrepreneur owning several businesses, continued to shower his generosity on his relatives, especially nieces and nephews, until his death in '83. The old Chadderton Airport has finally been developed into Linden Pointe Innovative Business Campus. It is a $6 million public-private economic development initiative between Kake Development of Hermitage (Fred George, principal), the City of Hermitage and the Commonwealth of Pennsylvania. One of its prime tenants is Cypress Semiconductor (NYSE: CY). Others are Butler County Community College and various doctors.

Richard "Dick" Mackell finished his first two years of the Holloway Plan at Grove City College. Dick relates, "Then I reported to flight training, and I got my wings in February of 1950. I stayed

Dick Mackell stands aboard the USS Saratoga CVA 60 in the Mediterranean Sea in 1964, having just landed the Douglas A-4 Skyhawk behind him.

in the Navy as a pilot, and went all over the world: from the Mediterranean to Antarctica to commanding a squadron in Vietnam in '66-'67. I retired in June of '69 with the rank of Navy Commander and haven't flown since. When I retired in '69, I was living in Florida. We moved back to Mercer in the mid '80s. After the Navy, I was in the heating and cooling business and also a city manager for H&R Block. Those lessons at Grove City Airport were a large part of the making of my career. That assurance of success begins with the proper start from an accomplished, professional instructor, such a person was Gardner Birch."

Board 3

Bill Mong, out of the Army, began at Grove City College in the fall of '48 and graduated in '52. With a degree in mechanical engineering, he soon went to work for Westinghouse Airbrake in Wilmerding, Pa., south of Monroeville and was there for 40 years. Since retiring in '93, he has joined the Erwin Male Chorus, formed in 1913, singing bass in their popular concert series.

Jim Rodgers had a varied working career over many years. He worked for the George J. Howe Company (he's pictured on a brochure they use), for a dairy, then a pie factory. He purchased "Good Pies" in Saegertown, baking 5,000 to 10,000 pies a day. In '76 he married, sold the company and moved to warmer North Carolina. Jim continued to work in a variety of jobs until in 2005 at age 81 he retired from being a porter for Carmax.

David Schmid graduated from Slippery Rock High in '49 and enlisted in the Navy the next day. He was a Navy Seabee, in heavy construction all over the world: Greece, Italy, Spain, Africa and Korea. For six days aboard a landing ship tank he helped put pontoons in Inchon Harbor. In a matter of days, starting on September 15, 1950, the highly successful invasion operation under Gen. Douglas MacArthur broke the back of the North Korean invasion of the South and liberated the city of Seoul. David next was in Cuba when Fidel Castro took over and then served two tours in Vietnam. He served in the Navy until '71, then went back to Petrolia, Pa., and worked for Witco for four years. With a drawl and a dry sense of humor, understated and modest David isn't quick to talk about himself. When asked what he does

with his time, his only response is that he mows his three-quarter-acre property with a push mower for exercise. But don't let that fool you; he can spout facts and details about the history and times of the Korean and Vietnam Wars that would put professors to shame. And he'll attend any event that involves the Solo Boards because he has a natural curiosity and an interest in important things.

How can one not rave about Ray "Rocky" Filer? A CEO of his own company who was able to retire early has met Rocky and said that a whole chapter could be written about him. Does that tell how special he is? Yet his humble beginnings and understated personality belie that. But who else at age 82 is waiting for the FAA to inspect the third airplane that he has personally built? And he built all three aircraft (wood, metal, fabric) in the modest impeccable brick rancher and garage that he built by hand starting in 1954. There are no diplomas on his walls, rather Wendell August Forge commemorative plates. But with his fine mind, his diligent work ethic and innate curiosity, there is not a lesson in life that he has not mastered.

Rocky returned from the war and eventually went to work in heavy equipment running a dragline for strip-mining. He describes the line as "a big boom that walks like a duck." Early in the '50s he worked for George Bobo then Allison Engineering for a total of 35 years, all this to support his family and his love of flying. He became a flight instructor and owned five planes that he restored. For years, he has been an active member of the EAA Chapter #161 in Grove City, having made numerous trips to Oshkosh, Wis., in his RV with his second plane in tow for Experimental

Aircraft Association's annual summer AirVenture. This is an annual migration of tens of thousands of general aviation enthusiasts who attend competitions, air shows, seminars and demonstrations and bask in the love of anything to do with planes.

The most recent venture began when Ray's wife, Anita, noticed that he was too quiet, lacked a project and needed something to do. Rocky got on the Internet and found an 18-year-old Kitfox kit for sale. Only the wing frames had been assembled. Similar in concept to the Piper J-3, a Kitfox is a lightweight, two-place fabric covered sport aircraft, easy to fly from short and unimproved airfields. In March of 2006, the couple got in their RV and drove to upper Michigan through several feet of snow, then towed the kit home. Like Rocky Balboa, Ray now had a familiar challenge: Could he do it one more time? No one who knows him would doubt it. It's done. Waiting to be inspected. Waiting for its maiden flight at the Grove City Airport. Ray and Anita, both in their second marriage, are quite a team. Their mutual respect, support, encouragement and affection are quiet les-

Rocky Filer built his second metal fabricated plane in the 1990s.

sons in wise love. She's right there for him and his flying, he's right there for her and her church work. They've set a record in my book: Rocky for building his third plane at age 82 and Anita for telling him to "go ahead and buy it."

Jack Mars took over running the airport at age 24. No doubt that because of his age and personality, it was run much looser than Gardner Birch ran it previously. The gang was a bit rowdier, pushed the limits further, created more stories and laughed harder under Jack. But there were no major detrimental incidents. Au contraire, there was a very nice happening!

The next farm over, separated by only a long slice of land, was owned by Caryl Starr, who had been a retail manager for Horne and Harter Department Stores. After retirement, he, his wife and daughter, Elaine, moved to the 86 acres in Grove City, where Caryl had long ago gone to college. Elaine worked at the drive-in and attended James Madison College in Virginia. After graduation, she took an elementary teaching job in Baltimore but spent summers back on the farm.

Looking for something interesting, she took a stroll down Airport Road to see the Fly Boys. It didn't take her long to fall for "Jack the Charmer." Even her students were smitten when he came to visit her classroom and told them about flying. He managed those getaways in addition to overseeing day-to-day operations, instructing and occasionally helping to sponsor a popular air show.

In 1952, when Cooper-Bessemer took over the airport, Jack needed another job. George Bobo let him take his plane for an interview with Beckett Aviation in Youngstown. Jack got

At Jack and Elaine Mars' wedding reception, the grin of best man Gardner Birch, far left, shows his approval of their marriage.

the position. Next was his biggest plunge of all. On April 11, 1953, Jack Mars married Elaine Starr at the Epiphany Episcopal Church in Grove City. Gardner Birch, wearing his Hickey Freeman suit from George Bobo, served as his best man. A small reception was held back at the farm, and the couple started married life in an apartment in Youngstown.

Beckett Aviation, which did contract work with small and large clients, moved Jack to Pittsburgh in 1956. Even then, he had a congenital nervous condition that caused his legs to tremor when he was stressed. George Lupinacci, head pilot for H.J. Heinz and co-pilot to Jack in the '70s, says, "In 1971 the Heinz Company was one of

Beckett's contracts. (Heinz) subsequently left and took the pilots from the gene pool that were recommended by Beckett." Jack began piloting for Heinz in '72, one of six pilots in three crews who flew nationally and internationally.

Dick Bailey remembers a time when Jack was working for Heinz. "He called and asked if I wanted to take a ride in a Lear Jet to Wyoming. I had crushed my arm and couldn't work, so I said yes. One of their big-shots had taken sick, and we had to go get him. Jack even let me fly the plane. Somewhere in Minnesota we needed to refuel. Jack said, 'They give green stamps down there' and landed. When we were full, a guy came out and threw a case in the plane. I asked, 'What's in

Pilot Jack Mars, left, and co-pilot Bob Derr flew the Heinz Company's Jetstar Dash 6 around 1973.

the case?' Jack stated, 'That's the case of green stamps.' It was actually a case of steaks that Jack shared with me, the big-shot and everybody."

Bob Derr flew co-pilot with Jack for Heinz for several years in the mid '70s before moving on to Delta Airlines. Bob says, "We were flying on a Gulf Stream 1—Jack, myself and Mr. Heinz. We were going back to Pittsburgh, and we hit some brutally turbulent weather. We forgot that Mr. Heinz was in the back. From back there we hear, 'Boy, I never had this much fun in all my life.'"

George Lupinacci recounts, "Heinz's flight department was a different animal (than Jack had experienced at Beckett). Seven years after the transition Heinz acquired new planes. Jack didn't make the cut and retired." Even 25 years later he remembers "that Jack sure liked his Canadian Club toddy."

Elaine didn't like the snowy winters, so in the '80s the two moved to Bartow, Fla. Jack joined the Civil Air Patrol and flew volunteer missions in a twin-engine plane looking for drug smugglers over the ocean. He began instructing and teaching through the CAP and returned a couple times a year to Grove City to visit his buddies. In the 1990s Jack was diagnosed with cancer and finally succumbed in August of '96. Elaine had a fatal stroke in March of '97. They are buried together in the Plain Grove Cemetery. The black onyx headstone is chiseled with a DC3 banking off into the sun, with the inscription, "He flew away ... and she followed."

James Fascetti worked at Westinghouse in Sharon until he retired in 1980. After several health problems, he died in March of 2006.

Bill Webster continued to be an avid hunter and gun collector: pistols, rifles and all kinds of guns. Chink Brandon often repaired them. Bill retired from Cooper-Bessemer and passed away in July of 1996.

Bob Hockenberry met a beautiful young girl from Ellwood City and they were married in September of 1950. Unfortunately, she had kept it hidden that at 14 she had a nervous breakdown. After the birth of their first son, she had to be institutionalized in Warren, Pa. Bob went to live with his parents who helped raise the son. Bill Raymer says, "During the 20 years she was in, Bob was straight as an arrow. Finally she was well enough to come home. Their son married and moved to Florida, got a good job and then committed suicide. Bob was never the same after that. He thought the son's wife had had him killed. Rocky helped Bob sell his Cessna 140A a month before he died in 1993."

Jim Hepler married in '52 and worked for Ford Motors. He became a motorcycle enthusiast with a Harley. In '60, he moved his family to Indianapolis, picked up his horn and started playing again. Often it was a gig on weekends. His son, David, a jazz pianist, remembers his dad. "He was a whistler, there was always a tune going on in his head. After dinner, he'd go downstairs and start to play; he liked playing as much as any trumpet player ever. In 1996, I played a New Year's Eve gig, and he played with me. When he died in January of 2004, we played his music at his funeral."

Good-looking Clarence "Ding Dong" Bell was always doing something crazy according to Jim Rodgers. "One day it was very windy and Clarence was flying a small plane into the wind. He throttled back, and those of us on the ground saw the plane actually fly backwards!" At the end of August 1953, Clarence was flying the Montgomery's DeHavilland Dove, back from Idlewild Airport in New York City. According to an eyewitness, the British ship, as it approached the Grove City Airport, appeared to be in trouble and was coming in without motors. Headlines from The Herald in Sharon, Pa., read, "Grove City Pilot And Fiancée Die In Crash." The paper continued, "A Grove City construction firm's plane crashed into a farm field while attempting a forced landing near Harrisville ... Pilot Clarence E. Bell, 33, of Clintonville, and his passenger, Miss Lydia Vera Grabe ... were thrown from the ship and died instantly. The plane, an eight-passenger twin-engine craft ... (had) both motors torn loose from their moorings as one wingtip touched the ground and forced the ship into a ground loop from low altitude, but it did not catch fire. Bell apparently had time to cut his ignition before the crash." Posy remembers, "Clarence had one engine shut down and the other was smoking when he was only three miles from the airport. He picked a field of decent size to put it down in, unfortunately he was headed toward the narrow side. In an attempt to save the plane, he tried to make a low turn toward the long way of the field. He dug in the wingtip and rolled it up like a ball. And so we lost a well-liked pilot."

The Herald in Sharon, Pa., covered the crash and deaths of Clarence Bell and his fiancée.

149

The paper continued, "President C.B. Montgomery placed the plane, used to transport executives and others to far-flung projects and operations, at a value of more than $100,000." C.B. Montgomery III, now president of Montgomery Truss and Panel, said, "In 1989, we sold the retail and now we only make trusses and wall panels." But the company still occupies the same building and location where his grandfather started the original business in 1920.

John Krofcheck has several enlistments in the service. He joined the National Guard and was an M.P. in security, first in military prisons, then in civilian prisons. In 1963, he returned to civilian life, going to work for Firestone as a credit manager in Hermitage, then Uniroyal, then National Life Insurance. He still lives in Hermitage.

When James Kennedy graduated from the Temple University School of Medicine in '52, he interned at Mercy Hospital in Pittsburgh. He went into private practice in Grove City for four or five months with two other doctors, but decided he wanted "to go west." Jim did one and a half years of training at Los Angeles Hospital. On family, he wryly comments, "I met my wife in prison. Actually it was on the 12th floor of the hospital, the prison ward, where she was a nurse." They settled in Davis, Calif., where Jim had a family practice and where they raised seven children. He retired in 1995 and flew occasionally until 2000.

Ed Black went to school at the Art Center College in Pasadena, Calif. He got drafted into the Army and was in photo operations. When he got out, he opened a photo studio in Grove City and later went into marketing for the Atlantic Oil Company. Though he has lived in Grove City all his life, he and his wife winter in Florida.

Salt-of-the-earth Bill Raymer, whose detailed mind is still as sharp as a tack, worked his adult life at Cooper-Bessemer on the midnight shift as a

Montgomery Truss and Panel still stands on West Main Street in Grove City today. It is the same building used by the original Montgomery Builders, where Clarence Bell worked as a pilot.

diesel tester. After retiring in '88, he drove a school bus. He owned four planes over the flying career that meant so much to him: the WACO bi-wing, a Cessna 172 he bought from George Monroe, a Piper Cherokee he owned with Gene Rodgers and an Aeronca Chief. He was flying this plane in '91 when the engine quit. He managed to land the plane on a highway near the Slippery Rock Airport, but he was thrown out of his seat and the wing was torn off. That was the last of his flying. Bill spoke to me personally about his crash— upfront, ego in check. No one else has stepped to the plate like this. I've heard of their crash from someone else. Bill, the modest man whose solid values guide him, still lives on Bessemer Avenue, within a short walk to the eerily silent Cooper-Bessemer plant.

Una Hart graduated from Grove City College with a degree in biology education. She taught English and history in Arnold, Pa., until she had children. She lives in Library, Pa., but still has her parents' home in Stoneboro, Pa.

Fred "Posy" Thompson, born in '21, was so upset after being told to leave the airport when Cooper-Bessemer leased it in '52 that he stopped flying for a few years and just worked in his floral wholesale business. Then in '62, "The Disease" resurfaced and he had to get off the ground again. He took up sailplane flying in Erie, Pa. "I still find sailplane flying the most satisfying way to assuage the cravings of my deep-seated affliction. In '65, I added a multi-engine rating and bought a Cessna 170. Then in '71 and for the next six years, I went to Paris, Texas, to fly the Big Iron (military aircraft). I loved to fly them, smell them, touch them and hear those mighty engines. So, even if

Uncle Sam wouldn't let me fly the Big Iron (during WWII), I managed it on my own, even though I was a little long in the tooth; 1975 turned into a banner year. I made my annual trip to Paris, Texas, bought a Myers Little Toot, got a seaplane rating and pulled the coup of my lifetime by getting a half-hour dual in the Goodyear Blimp. I had talked my way into the co-pilot seat. After ascending, he said, 'Do you want to fly this thing?' I couldn't say 'yes' fast enough. He asked if I could hold 500 feet. I said I would try mightily. With that, he got out of his seat and I got into it with great speed, lest he change his mind. He wanted

Posy Thompson and his Junkers CL-1, the last of eight aircraft he owned. Note the machine gun in the back cockpit and the bomb between the landing gear wheels. This photo was published in a magazine with the title 'Men and Their Toys.'

to fly down the coast, then inland. I can't recall the landmarks, but I remember they were highly visible. I was paying strict attention, not wishing to get caught in the student's dilemma when the instructor says, 'Take us back home.' And he did! And I did! It was a perfect day to fly a blimp: clear and with negligible wind and no noticeable thermals. Flying that triangle was surely a satisfying experience. My pilot friend then made an entry in my logbook, 'Thirty minutes dual in N1A.'"

Young in mind and body, Posy, who lives in Erie, Pa., continued, "I am 85 years old and satisfied with my life. I tried not to miss anything. I golf, ride my bicycle, downhill ski, bowl and take care of a one-acre yard. I pilot a state-owned 20-passenger boat on the bay and serve as a guide on a replica of the Brig Niagara, Perry's War of 1812 flagship. I am happily married to a beautiful lady, Donnie, who makes my life easy and worth living. I flew for 62 years. I started at age 15 and gave it up at 77. I was privileged to get checked out in 45 different aircraft and to own eight planes." Aviation was privileged to have Posy.

Board 4

Robert "Scotty" Scott, the mechanic, took a position with North American Aviation as a tech rep on Naval experimental aircraft at Patuxent, Md. His project was the AJ-2 Fury, the Navy's version of the F-86 Saber. North American moved him to Gulfport, Miss., then to California, and he retired out of the home office in Columbus, Ohio. Posy continues his thoughtful eulogy of Scotty, "He tired of loafing and took a job with General Electric in Erie. That's how I got to Erie. We had always been enamored with Ryan Aircraft—the 'Spirit of St. Louis' was a Ryan. I found a Ryan in a barn in Meadville. I called Scotty and asked him if he remembered saying that he would work on a Ryan for free. He said 'yes' and I said, 'Get ready, 'cause I'm bringing one up.' That began a seven-year odyssey and I finally moved the Ryan and myself to Erie. During one of those trips, I met my dear Donnie. So good friend Scotty was responsible for my two great loves. Scotty had a fine 26-foot Erickson sailboat that we raced on Sundays at the Erie Yacht

Posy Thompson bought this Ryan PT-22 that Robert 'Scotty' Scott restored. Gardner Birch also bought the same model plane and had Scotty restore it.

Club. Sadly, Scotty died (in 2005) and is buried in Moneta, Va."

After his flying lessons, Harry Stine was in the Air Force Reserves and was called up during the Korean War. After that he went to work for the government's Department of Logistics. He retired in '72. Eight years ago he fell on black ice and suffered memory loss.

Clarence "Sam" Pearson worked his adult life for Cooper-Bessemer as a crane operator and assemblyman. Bill Raymer tells that "the 1960s got a hold of him: long hair, pony tail, somewhat of an outlaw." Clarence had three marriages and

Clarence Pearson enjoys a March 2005 pilot reunion.

got into car racing, too. After some illness, Clarence died in October '05.

The Army and the Korean War kept Dick Double busy until '52. When he got back to Grove City, the PA-12 that he owned with Birch had been sold. Later that year, he moved to Long Beach, Calif., where his mother was living. He enrolled in the University of Southern California and earned a degree in mechanical engineering. He accepted a position with the city of Long Beach in the oil department. He spent the next 33 years there, and when he retired around '90, he was in charge of all production and drilling work. But that was only his day job. Nights and weekends were for flying. Dick taught some 2,500 students basic ground school for 20 years at night at Long Beach City

College and the Torrance Adult School. He has given more than 4,000 hours of instrument flight instruction and several thousand hours of basic flight instruction. Many of his students are working for the airlines. Dick himself has nearly 9,000 hours flight time. Dick purchased a Cessna 182P (N7021Q) almost 30 years ago that he keeps in his own hangar. Close friend Barbara, a former student who has 1,200 of her own hours, and he are a team who have made many flights to Baha, Mexico; the East Coast; Alaska to above the Artic Circle; and Monument Valley, just to name a few. He keeps his mind sharp with frequent workouts on the computer; he can burn a CD, e-mail or research airplane ownership history. Dick's love

of flying as he approaches age 80 is as strong as ever and he still annually attends the Aircraft Owners and Pilots Association (AOPA) convention.

Fuzzy DeArment left Grove City in February of '47 with the new car, the Piper Cub and willowy 20-year-old Fern Hagen. He moved to Sioux Falls, Iowa. In October Martha DeArment moved to Greenville, Pa., and went to work for the hospital. Daughter Ella May, who said her mother was bitter, never got the promise from Fuzzy that he would teach her to fly when she was 16. His contact was limited to two additional visits in her life. One came after Ella's first husband died and left her with four children. Fuzzy, who had married

Dick Double and his friend, Barbara, stand in front of Dick's Cessna 182P that he has owned for 30 years. The N7021Q has a new interior, all the latest goodies and gadgets, and resides in a hangar that Dick owns in Long Beach, Calif. In July 2007 Dick marked 62 years of having a pilot's license.

Fern and had another daughter, came and asked to borrow some of the insurance money. At age 62, he was living in Madison, Wis., working as a salesman for the Reliable Life and Casualty Company. Fuzzy, always a heavy smoker, developed lung cancer, then a brain tumor, and died in 1974. Martha, who provided his photo album for this project, is in her '90s, quick to remember and still lives in Greenville.

Fred Lynn worked his adult life in the accounting department of Cooper-Bessemer and retired in 1986. Around 2000, he got to fly a new Cessna. He hadn't flown in a very long time and said, "It was great!"

After he soloed, Ellis Klingensmith went to work for Cooper-Bessemer for a short time, then went to Grove City College and became a guidance counselor in Ashtabula, Ohio, where he still lives. He bought a Cessna 140 and also owned a Piper Cherokee that he sold in '81. Now his planes are smaller; he builds and flies models and has entered them in the "Top Gun" model competition in Florida.

Fonnie Bailey's work ethic ran so deep that he continued to work until he was 84 years old. After the war, he began to drive a coal truck for Bowie Coal. Next he drove a bus for Brenton Holter, then a bus for Continental Trailways and, finally, a truck for a milk transport company. He says he would still be driving, but a shoulder injury in 2004 forced him into retirement. Though he never flew, several of the pilots are still his good friends.

John Bailey came back from Europe and worked in a coal mine and then in a steel mill in Warren, Ohio, and lived in nearby Cortland. He and brother Jim started jumping with parachutes

Dick Bailey poses with his '58 Pontiac that he raced on the beach at Daytona in 1958.

in the early '60s. John died in 2002.

Dick Bailey likes speed and engines. Thus he started racing NASCAR in 1950 at the old Daytona Beach raceway. In '59 he raced at the Daytona International Speedway in the Sportsman and Modified Division. In '68 he raced at the Florida State Fair, finally stepping out of the driver's seat around 1980. Dick kept up with his flying, too. He, two others and Bill Raymer bought a Cessna 172 Skyhawk from George Monroe. A picture of Dick during his racing days is hanging in the Heinz History Center's Western Pennsylvania Sports Museum in Pittsburgh. But there is more to Dick than his past, which included a 44-year career at Cooper-Bessemer. His present life includes a two- to three-month winter trip to New Orleans to work. At the mouth of the Mississippi River, a dredge with four Cooper-Bessemer engines is brought in annually for Dick's inspection and possible repair. The skills he learned long ago in Grove City still provide for him at age 84. In today's "use and toss" culture, the quality of those original, surviving engines and the depth of Dick's work ethic boggles the mind.

Fred Bailey had lingering effects of his stomach wound even while learning to fly. He went to work in a limestone plant and didn't fly much. He married and had kids, then moved to Lake Worth, Fla., where he died in 1967.

Jim Bailey would make the military his career and see three wars: WWII in the Navy infantry, the Korean War as a paratrooper and Vietnam as a helicopter pilot. He lived in many U.S. locations getting extensive training and checking out in 15 aircraft. According to his only daughter, Joyce,

"He took his flying very serious." He was even a helicopter pilot for President Eisenhower. Jim was on his third tour of duty in Vietnam when, in October of 1969 during a monsoon, the rotor blade hit a tree and the chopper went down in a river. He was missing a year, a month and a day before he was declared dead. The family chartered a bus from Brenton Holter and went to his funeral at Arlington National Cemetery. Two years later the chopper was found in the river, and Jim's flight boot and pistol were recovered.

Helicopter pilot Jim Bailey served thee tours of duty in Vietnam.

Board5

Ed Fitzgerald got his private pilot's license in '47. He later worked for a machine shop in Grove City and a Chrysler shop in New Castle. He rounded that out with 30 years as a rural mail carrier. Ed lives in Volant, Pa.

Dr. Ed Dicola became a surgeon in the Erie area. He died in January of 2004.

Dr. Salvatore "Sal" Pisciotto, or "Dr. Sal" as he was called by all his patients, returned to New York and set up family practice. He did some flying in East Hampton, but then found a new love — boating. He bought a 39-foot Bertram and ventured into deep-sea fishing near Montauk with his sons. He still had an active practice when he died at 74 in 1996.

George Bobo was flying high after he got his private license, not only in aviation but in all aspects of his life. Coal profits had bought him the respect that had eluded him in his early years. He was a member and past president of the elite Grove City Country Club. Life couldn't get any better, and, to his credit, he valued and rewarded anyone connected with his success. He never forgot from whence he came. In November of '52, Rocky Filer, who was temporarily out of work but had his commercial pilot license, posed to George, "Why don't you take me on as your personal pilot?" George replied, "For all the flying I do, I can do it myself."

A few weeks later, George Bobo determined he would provide a joyous Christmas to his family of origin in Kentucky. On December 23, 1952, George climbed into "Baby," his Beechcraft Bonanza, loaded like Santa, to visit his mother and take an abundance of Christmas gifts to his nieces and nephews. He then planned to visit friends after landing in Gratz, Ky. On arriving in the area, he flew low to buzz the house to let them know to come to the airport. Newspaper headlines told of the tragic catastrophe. One report cited engine failure, one implied pilot error. The bottom line was that Baby crashed to the ground not far from the house. The plane did not catch fire, but Bobo was found dead when rescuers reached the wreckage. He left a wife and three sons and is buried in the Crestview Cemetery in Grove City.

Fellow coal operator Ray Bowie, whose daughter went on to marry George's son, eulogized, "He was a good family man who spared no expense in making his family happy. This man, a one in a million, was made by our Maker and

Grove City Mine Owner Dies When His Plane Crashes

Rent Controls Lifted Again In This Area

Only Restrictions Now In Municipalities Which Asked For Them

The fluctuating status of rent controls for many Mercer County municipalities and townships swung toward the "off" side again yesterday when the federal government voided a previous ruling that had classified the county as a

George Z. Bobo

George Bobo Killed On Trip To Kentucky

Holiday Trip Ends Fatally Near Home Of Former Local Couple

George Z. Bobo, 200 Washington Blvd., Grove City, was instantly killed yesterday at 3:30 p. m. when his airplane crashed near Pleasureville, Ky.

He was 42 years old and was well known in western

A crash brought George Bobo's flying days to a tragic end.

Dick and Ralph Double stand in front of Grauman's Chinese Theater in Hollywood around 1954. One of the most famous movie theaters in the world, it is now part of the Hollywood and Highland Center, which is also home to the Kodak Theatre, site of the Academy Awards.

Master, however, after using the mold only once, he destroyed the mold and there will be none other like him." The courts controlled the Bobo estate, but allowed eldest son George Robert (Board 5), age 21, to take charge of the company. Even with loyal employees, the task was beyond Bob's ability. Bobo Coal went broke in 1964. A local legend and era had passed, never to return.

Ralph Double, Dick's dad, continued to work at Cooper-Bessemer, the only employer he ever knew. In the early '60s, he had a heart attack. Two years later at age 60, he had a second one and died.

Tall and good-looking, Ed McCarl went into the Navy in July of '48 after he soloed and also served in the Korean War. He spent 40 years as an electrician in commercial and industrial construc-

tion, all over from Maryland to New Jersey. He retired in Jackson Center, Pa., in '91. Though he was fit and youthful, he came down with a virulent form of pneumonia and died at age 76 on July 4, 2006.

Calvin Feather got out of the service and went to work for George Bobo. Even after Bobo's death, Cal stayed on as mine superintendent until 1963. The coal was stripped out locally, and the mines were closing. So he opened a gas station in Grove City on Broad Street. In '79 he went to work for Reznor Manufacturing in Mercer. Founded in 1888, Reznor makes residential and commercial heating units and is still in business today. Cal retired from there in '90 and still puts flowers on George Bobo's grave each year.

Al McDeavitt was a block and bricklayer all his life. He and his son went to Florida to work. He died around 1990. Brother Buck first tried farming, then spent almost 20 years as a welder in Butler. Now at the age of 83, he is farming on 73 acres in West Liberty. He has a herd of 35 cattle that are a cross of White Face and Angus. He farms another piece of land, too, and grows corn, oats and hay. Farmers and gardeners renew each spring when seeing the first green shoots of hope push out of the ground. That will keep Buck farming for years into the future.

Jack McNutt worked most of his life as a bus driver, traveling to every continental state over 64 years and logging more than 3 million miles. In 1965, he and Fonnie Bailey worked seven days a week for a year. As Jack said, "There were buses that needed drivers and no one else to drive them." Jack went back to occasional truck driving, but mainly worked for Anderson, Fullington and Trailways. In '91, he pulled back to part-time and retired in 2006. Jack attended the Board reunion in March of 2005 but lost a battle with cancer in February of 2007.

Canny Fin and Maxine Wilson sustained their modest lifestyle from the three airports they created. Through high and low economic times, Fin had sense to adjust to what needed to be adjusted to get him through a bad time. He could stretch a dollar, tighten his belt, say "no" and always sell the positive. In the 1950s, the golden income from all war programs had all dried up. He leased the Grove City Airport to Cooper-Bessemer, guaranteeing a very reliable stream of cash flow. He sold the New Castle Airport to the City of New Castle. The city formed an Airport Authority and in '97 turned the property over to the Lawrence County Airport Authority. Haski Aviation has been the fixed base operator at the New Castle Airport since 1973. Fin took the proceeds from the sale of his first airport to Islamorada, Fla., the fourth island in the Florida Keys. There, the Wilsons built the Blue Fin Lodge, which they operated for eight years, and began deep-sea fishing. During this time he made his last flight to the Bahamas. Tired of a 24/7 work schedule, they sold the Florida motel.

In 1963, Ed Chadderton bought the Chadderton Airport in Sharon for $40,000. Missing flying but prohibited by cost, Fin joined the Quiet Birdmen in 1977. No doubt he told many an embellished story to his fellow pilots about his accomplishments. His last move in the game of entrepreneurship was in 1981. He sold the Grove Airport for $150,000. With that cushion, the

Three-time airport developer Fin Wilson is full of life at 77.

Wilsons ended their twilight years wintering on Islamorada and summering in Princeton, Pa., in a mobile home on the old Wilson family homestead.

Gardner Birch returned to the security of bricklaying and its unions. He didn't hate bricklaying, but he hated that it tore up his hands, his back and his mind. On the surface, he adjusted with new activities and projects. He joined a barbershop quartet, built a two-car garage with a cement driveway and later a large family room with a fireplace onto the Birch home in Hermitage. He also took the family on that long-denied fishing trip to Kahshe Lake in Canada, hunted more often and loaded his own shotgun shells.

But when alone, his mind drifted back to the most wonderful time in his life. And he felt a disappointment and discouragement that his wife had not supported him. Though normally quite talkative, he rarely spoke further about flying or the airport. According to Bill Raymer, Gardner did rent a plane at the Chadderton Airport and took three friends to a baseball game in Cleveland. He kept up with the airport gang, occasionally hunting or visiting. He was best man in Jack Mars' wedding. Gardner Birch, #66923, renewed his CAA Certification in 1947 and in 1951 applied for an Airman Identification Card. That was his last contact with the CAA.

In 1953, there was a major family event. Grace became pregnant and gave birth to twin boys—prematurely. Though it was a big added financial responsibility (five children from 0 to 13), everyone was delighted with the addition of infants Jim and Gardner. Birch responded by enlarging the house. He headed the building of the first Little League dugout and new ball field in Hermitage. He took time monthly to cut his elderly uncle's hair. Family was important. Grace responded by enrolling at Youngstown State College and getting her teaching degree at night. Later, she started teaching first grade in Sharpsville. Family life was busy, normal and well in control with the three girls in their mid- to late-teens and the twins in elementary school.

In July of 1962, Birch took a union job for Eichleay Corporation, a Pittsburgh heavy industrial contractor. Eichleay was relining Sharon Steel's No. 2 blast furnace, a furnace that had been idle for two years. The job was scheduled for completion in December of '62. Local headlines on October 16 reported, "On Monday, one of the worst industrial accidents in history of the Shenango Valley happened. A three-and-a-half-ton steel plate broke loose from its rigging and plunged 50 feet into a blast furnace, killing two workmen and injuring six others at the Sharon Steel Corp. Roemer Works. Killed were Gardner Birch, age 52, a bricklayer, who died of internal hemorrhage, fractured sternum and abdominal and thoracic contusions, and Graham Matthews, a

laborer, who died of a crushed chest, internal injuries, internal hemorrhage and abdominal and thoracic injuries. The plate, which measured 3.5 feet by 3.5 feet, broke loose carrying with it parts of the shattered scaffolding. The heavy steel plate crashed through two different elevations of heavy wooden beam and steel scaffolding, with a deafening roar into the bottom of the furnace where Birch and Matthews and five others were working. The two men were killed instantly."

The bonds of friendship from the airport, even 14 years later, assured that some of the airport gang would show their respect by attending Birch's funeral. Those friends in attendance were Bill Raymer, Pete Walters, Bob Hockenberry and Jack and Elaine Mars. Grace did not cope well with Gardner's death. As in her childhood, she felt victimized and let alcohol comfort her. She taught school until 1980 and retired. After a second reoccurrence of colon cancer, she died in January of 1995.

When Birch left, the airport chugged along under Mars until being leased by Cooper-Bessemer in '52. Not only was it used for Lefebvre's pleasure, but it offered inventory storage for the company, too. Gordon, and possibly George Bobo, paved the runways. Men with money were now in, the regular guys were out. Then disaster struck both men. First Bobo was killed piloting his own plane. Three years later, Lefebvre fell victim to a bad bottom line and to the hostility of the board of directors, who he tangled with one too many times. He was forced out via sudden resignation.

In the 1960s, Cooper-Bessemer subleased part of the property to August, Menzies and Monroe, three local, avid pilots. Bob August was owner of Wendell August Forge, a nationally known forge still in business in Grove City today. Originally it specialized in architectural detail pieces and now its focus is giftware. Two of its pieces are on display at the National Museum of American History of the Smithsonian Institute. Bill Menzies was a well-known local doctor. George Monroe was a high-level supervisor at Cooper-Bessemer. He began his flying in a blimp in WWI. George and his wife had no children, a result of mumps during the war. Thus he could afford the expensive hobby. He owned several planes, including an Aeronca Chief and a Cessna 172.

Development began in the 1970s for a new airport for Grove City, one more modern and more central to major transportation. The Grove City Airport (29D) on Oakley Kelly Drive off Route 208 at Interstate 79 opened in the mid 1970s. The Borough of Grove City owns the airport and leases out the aviation operations. In 2007, it was leased to Steve Rhule and Doug Thomas. The neglected old airport's fate was sealed. In 1981, after 40 years of squeezing every penny he could out of the operation, Findley Wilson sold the property to Lucas Coal Co., which later became Magnum

Minerals, at a price of $150,000 for strip-mining. Now the earth would literally be dug open by monstrous, deafening equipment to scavenge for chunks of fuel that could be sold. Before the hangar was dozed down, someone, possibly Gene Harman, noticed the Boards still hanging on the wall. Perceptively, they were removed and because of the watchful eye of the local EAA Chapter #161, now hang at Grove City Airport.

After ravaging the land for 11 years, Magnum had no more use for it and put it up for sale at a fraction of its original cost. The second private buyer paid in the low $40,000s. It was then sold in 1999 to Richard Beech, vice president of the George J. Howe Company. Dick is the grandson of George Howe and the son of Pete Beech (who offered Jack McNutt his job back). The almost-adjoining Starr farm had its farmhouse torn down and was strip-mined, too. The old cement block drive-in to the north on Route 58 amazingly still stands. The area where the cars parked facing a huge white painted wall is now a pasture that animals share with speaker posts. The McCoy farmhouse is now back in family lineage, but conveyed from the bloodline by divorce. Fortunately, owner Floy McCoy, who works for Grove City College, appreciates its history. She has stoned the exterior and the small carryout once used to sell lunches to the cadets is still standing. Under a large tree in the backyard, she has left a cement block half buried—the corner stone of one wall of the airport—as a salute to times gone by there. Across the street, new homes are being constructed in an eastwardly direction, like houses being added on a Monopoly board.

The topography of the old airport is notice-

New signage welcomes visitors to the Grove City Airport.

Floy McCoy kept true the integrity of the McCoy farmhouse.

Fledgling pilots received a diploma when they soloed in a Piper Cub at the Grove City Airport, after which their names were inscribed on the Boards.

Rocky Filer stands in front of the old north-south runway at the original Grove City Airport.

ably lower than the adjoining McCoy farm, a visual confirmation of the raping of the land. No one knows what zoning regulations would be required for any future use, if there is one. The land sits quiet and serene, healing itself. Scrub grass and tall weeds now cover its surface. You can still see the pattern of the old runways. A pond has formed in the back, with amazingly clear water that provides for fishing on a lazy summer day. If you know right where to look,

there is still a small section of the runway intact. Posy laments, "When I get down to Grove City, I sometimes drive past the old airfield and sadly contemplate the empty spot where the hangar stood. I faintly hear the engine noise and in my mind's eye see the airplanes and my old friends."

These friends shared a love of flying at that treasured airport where as fledgling pilots they learned to fly proud.

A reunion of Board pilots in March 2005 brought together, seated from left, Ray Cornelius, Bill Raymer, Evelyn Kreidle, Chuck Dickey, Dick Bailey; standing from left, Bob McGowan, David Schmid, Fred 'Posy' Thompson, Ed Fitzgerald, Daniel 'Buck' McDeavitt, Jack McNutt, Ray 'Rocky' Filer, Bill Mong and Ed McCarl.

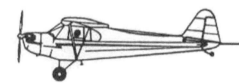

They Flew Proud!

BIBLIOGRAPHY

Books

Bates, Samuel. *History of Erie County, Pa.* (1884)

Brinkley, Douglas. *The WWII Memorial* (Smithsonian Books 2004)

Grove City College. *Ouija* (yearbooks for 1943 and 1944)

Keller, David. *Cooper Industries 1833-1983* (Ohio University Press 1983)

Mercer County Historic Society. *Mercer County Pa. Pictorial History 1800-2000* (Donning 2001)

Pisano, Dominick. *To Fill the Skies with Pilots* (University of Illinois Press 1993)

Documents

Army Air Force *Station Historical Report of the 8th College Training Detachment, Grove City College, Grove City, Pa. March 1, 1943 to March 1, 1944*

Death Certificate from State of Pennsylvania for Baby Birch

Epilogue of Grove City College by Dr. Richard Jewell 2007

FAA personal file for Gardner Birch

Homelly, Henry. *History of the Grove City Volunteer Fire Department*

Selected documents from the Civil Aeronautic Administration to the Civilian Pilot Training Program from the Milne Special Collection and Archives at the University of New Hampshire

The McNair Papers, Institute for National Strategic Studies

Unpublished paper on Mercer County Mine History by Raymond Bowie and Harold Johnson

Organizations

Air Force Historical Research Agency, Maxwell Air Force Base, Alabama

Crawford County (Pa.) Historical Society, Anne Stewart Library

Federal Aviation Administration

Greenville (Pa.) Area Historical Society

Grove City (Pa.) Area Historical Society

Mercer County Historical Society

United States Military Academy at West Point

University of New Hampshire Archives

Publications

2000 Census-U.S. Census Bureau

AOPA Magazine, October 2005

Army Air Force Training Material, Flight Table

The Collegian, Grove City College

Cooper-Bessemer News

Flyin' Rapier (student newspaper of the 329th Detachment of Slippery Rock College), November 1943

Grove City College Bulletin, Alumni Issue

Grove City Reporter-Herald

The Herald, Sharon, Pa.

New Castle News, New Castle, Pa.

Piper Cub Special J3C-65 Owners Manual, 1946

The Vindicator, Youngstown, Ohio

Web Sites

www.airfields-freeman.com

www.airforcehistory.hq.af.mil

www.americanpresident.org

www.aviationhistory.com

www.aviationresourcehistory-geocities.com

www.centennialofflight.gov

www.educationnews.org

www.feri.org (The Franklin & Eleanor Roosevelt
     Institute)

www.gcc.edu (Grove City College)

www.gibill.va.gov

www.greatachievements.org

www.historyplace.com

www.history.sandiego.edu

www.homeofheroes.com

www.landings.com

www.learner.org

www.mhric.org (Mid-Hudson Regional
     Information Center)

www.microsoft.com

www.nationalpostalmuseum.com

www.penwomanship.com

www.stripes.com

www.usma.edu (United States Military Academy
     at West Point)

www.wikipedia.org

Interviews

Bailey, Fonnie; Bailey, John; Bailey, Joyce; Black, Edison; Bobo, Philip; Bovard, Margaret Fithian; Briner, Betty; Brydon, Sam; Chadderton, Paul; Cornelius, Ray; Creighton, John; Curletta, Caryl Starr; Davidson, Jeanne Carruthers; DeArment, Martha; Derr, Bob; Dickey, Chuck; Dicola, Nancy; Double, Dick; Erb, Ralph; Fascetti, Hilda; Feather, Calvin; Filer, Ray "Rocky"; Finney, Shari; Fitzgerald, Ed; Fry, Bob; Gaborski, Pat; Harris, Louise; Hart, Una; Haski, Martin; Heatley, Bertha "Birdy" Mueller; Heinberg, Beatrice; Henderson, David; Henderson, Helen; Hepler, David; Hoffman, Edith Kinder; Hoover, George; Jewell, Dr. Richard G.; Kemp, Hillis; Kennedy, James; Klingensmith, Ellis; Kreidle, Evelyn; Krofcheck, John; Lowers, Paul; Lupinacci, George; Lynn, Fred; Mackell, Dick; Maitland, Andy; Mars, Ric; McCarl, Ed; McCoy, Floy; McDeavitt, Dan "Buck"; McGowan, Bob; McNutt, Jack; Menzie, Bill; Miller, Don; Mong, Bill; Montgomery, C.B.; Neel, John; Nelson, Muriel "Dottie"; Pearson, Clarence "Sam"; Pisciotto, Marie; Raymer, Bill; Rodgers, Jim; Schmid, David; Scott, Robert "Scotty"; Stine, Nancy; Strange, Jim; Susi, Joe; Thompson, Dorothy; Thompson, Fred "Posy"; Webster, Bessie; Williamson, Eleanor; Zedreck, Verna

Statistics of World War II
(Including European and Pacific Theaters)

Countries	Total Deaths	% of Pre-War Pop.	Military Deaths	Civilian Deaths
USSR	20,600,000	10.4%	13,600,000	7,000,000
CHINA	10,000,000	2.0%		
GERMANY	6,850,000	9.5%	3,250,000	3,600,000
POLAND	6,123,000	17.2%	123,000	6,000,000
JAPAN	2,000,000	2.7%		
YUGOSLAVIA	1,706,000	10.9%		
FRANCE	810,000	1.9%	340,000	470,000
GREECE	520,000	7.2%		
UNITED STATES	500,000	0.4%	500,000	
AUSTRIA	480,000	7.2%		
ROMANIA	460,000	3.4%		
HUNGARY	420,000	3.0%		
ITALY	410,000	0.9%	330,000	80,000
CZECHOSLOVAKIA	400,000	2.7%		
GREAT BRITAIN	388,000	0.8%	326,000	62,000
NETHERLANDS	210,000	2.4%	198,000	12,000
BELGIUM	88,000	1.1%	76,000	12,000
FINLAND	84,000	2.2%		
AUSTRALIA	39,000	0.3%		
CANADA	34,000	0.3%		
ALBANIA	28,000	2.5%		
INDIA	24,000	0.01%		
NORWAY	10,262	0.3%		
NEW ZEALAND	10,000	0.6%		
LUXEMBOURG	5,000	1.7%		
TOTAL	**52,199,262**			

Stars, Bars, and a Circle

Were you around military installations in the 1941-1942 era? If you nod assent to this question, chances are you can recall the old star wing markings on military aircraft.

For 22 years this red, white, and blue insignia together with a striped tail rudder was representative of American airpower. But in World War II, it was discovered by pilots in early combat in the Pacific that it too closely resembled the markings on Japanese aircraft. Of more personal importance to these airmen, however, was the fact that it afforded an excellent bull's-eye for enemy pilots and gunners to draw a bead on. The Japanese marking, dubbed "meatball," was the blood-red circle depicting the rising sun.

Japan showed no sign of setting their rising sun, so on August 18, 1942, an order was issued to alter the U. S. insignia and to discontinue the display of stripes on the rudder. At this time only the red ball was eliminated from the design, and the insignia remained a white star on a round field of blue.

During 1943 an evaluation group at the Proving Ground at Eglin Field, Fla., determined in tests that the insignia was still confusing to airmen and advocated

that white bars be added on each side of the star. This change was authorized in orders of June 30 that year. In September 1943, the red border was changed to blue in an effort to eliminate all remaining confusion with enemy insignia.

At the end of the war another study on insignia was undertaken and a recommendation was adopted to reinstate the red in the marking. Thus in an authorization in 1947, two small horizontal red bars were added to the center of the side bars. This red, white, and blue device is still the wing and fuselage marking displayed on all aircraft and many missiles of the U. S. Air Force, Army, Navy, Marine Corps, and Coast Guard.

—Capt. WIRT D. GRIGGS

Courtesy of Air Force Historical Research Agency

Colleges participating in the CPTP '43-'44

(Listed by state, all participated in 1943 and 1944 unless otherwise noted.)

Institution	City	Detachment
Alabama		
Birmingham Southern College	Birmingham	017
Spring Hill College	Spring Hill	335
Tuskegee Institute	Tuskegee	320
University of Alabama	Tuscaloosa	057
Arkansas		
Arkansas State College	Jonesboro	079
Henderson State Teachers College	Arkadelphia	066
Ouachita College	Arkadelphia	067
University of Arkansas	Fayetteville	305
Arizona		
Arizona State Teachers College	Tempe	316
Colorado		
University of Denver	Denver	353
Florida		
University of Florida	Gainesville	062
University of Tampa	Tampa	018
Georgia		
Berry College	Mount Berry	001
Middle Georgia College	Cochran	050
Iowa		
Coe College	Cedar Rapids	306
Drake University	Des Moines	345
Iowa State Teachers College	Cedar Falls	080
Iowa Wesleyan College	Mount Pleasant	082
Morningside College	Sioux City	081
Idaho		
College of Idaho	Caldwell	311
Illinois		
Augustana College & Seminary	Rock Island	068
James Millikin University	Decatur	077
Knox College	Galesburg	302
Southern Illinois Normal University	Carbondale	069

Institution	City	Detachment
Indiana		
Butler University	Indianapolis	052
Indiana Central College*	Indianapolis	019
Kansas		
Fort Hays Kansas State College	Hays	083
Kansas State College of A & AS	Manhattan	100
Kansas State Teachers College	Emporia	084
Municipal University of Wichita	Wichita	085
Kentucky		
Centre College of Kentucky	Danville	020
Transylvania College	Lexington	322
Western Kentucky State Teachers College	Bowling Green	321
Louisiana		
Centenary College	Shreveport	086
Massachusetts		
Massachusetts State College	Amherst	058
Springfield College	Springfield	323
Maine		
Colby College	Waterville	021
Michigan		
Albion College	Albion	070
Michigan College of M&T	Houghton	098
Michigan State College of A&AS	East Lansing	310
Minnesota		
Macalester College	St. Paul	347
St. Cloud Teachers College	St. Cloud	071
St. John's University	Collegeville	087
State Teachers College	Moorhead	346
University of Minnesota	Minneapolis	088
Missouri		
Drury College	Springfield	340
Jefferson College	St. Louis	341
Rockhurst College	Kansas City	072
Southwestern Missouri State Teachers College	Springfield	099
University of Missouri	Columbia	307
Washington University	St. Louis	342
Mississippi		
Mississippi State College	State College	064

Institution	City	Detachment
Montana		
Montana State College	Bozeman	312
Montana State University	Missoula	317
North Carolina		
Catawba College	Salisbury	327
Davidson College	Davidson	024
Elon College	Elon	325
High Point College	High Point	326
North Carolina State College	Raleigh	059
North Dakota		
Jamestown College	Jamestown	303
University of North Dakota	Grand Forks	304
Nebraska		
Creighton University	Omaha	089
Hastings College	Hastings	073
Nebraska State Teachers College	Wayne	349
University of Nebraska	Lincoln	348
New Hampshire		
St. Anselm's College	Manchester	002
Nevada		
University of Nevada	Reno	313
New York		
Canisius College	Buffalo	022
Niagara University	Niagara	016
Rochester Business Institute	Rochester	051
State Teachers College	Oswego	324
Syracuse University	Syracuse	065
University of Buffalo	Buffalo	023
Ohio		
Capitol University	Columbus	005
Fenn College	Cleveland	053
Hiram College	Hiram	004
Kent State University	Kent	336
Marietta College	Marietta	025
Mount Union College	Alliance	026
University of Akron	Akron	003
University of Cincinnati	Cincinnati	029
University of Toledo	Toledo	027
Western Reserve University	Cleveland	028
Wittenberg College	Springfield	054
Xavier University	Cincinnati	030

Institution	City	Detachment
Oklahoma		
East Central State College	Ada	343
Northwest State Teachers College	Alva	092
Oklahoma A & M College	Stillwater	090
Oklahoma Baptist University	Shawnee	091
Oklahoma City University	Oklahoma City	344
University of Tulsa	Tulsa	074
Oregon		
Eastern Oregon College of Education	La Grande	354
Pennsylvania		
Albright College	Reading	007
Allegheny College	Meadville	031
Clarion State Teachers College	Clarion	337
Dickinson College	Carlisle	032
Duquesne University	Pittsburgh	328
Geneva College	Beaver Falls	036
Gettysburg College	Gettysburg	055
Grove City College	Grove City	008
Kutztown Teachers College	Kutztown	338
Lafayette College	Easton	034
Penn State College	State College	330
St. Vincent College	Latrobe	033
Slippery Rock State Teachers College	Slippery Rock	329
Susquehanna University	Selinsgrove	035
University of Pittsburgh	Pittsburgh	060
Waynesburg College	Waynesburg	009
Wilkes College	Wilkes-Barre	006
Williamsport & Dickinson Junior College	Williamsport	331
South Carolina		
Clemson College	Clemson	037
Erskine College	Due West	038
Furman University	Greenville	339
Presbyterian College	Clinton	039
Winthrop College	Rock Hill	041
Wofford College	Spartanburg	040
South Dakota		
Black Hills Teachers College	Spearfish	093
Tennessee		
Cumberland University	Lebanon	010
George Peabody College	Nashville	333
King College	Bristol	332
Marysville College	Marysville	042
Memphis State College*	Memphis	043
Middle Tennessee State College	Murfreesboro	011

Institution	City	Detachment
Tennessee (continued)		
Southwestern University of Tennessee	Memphis	013
State Teachers College	Johnson City	012
Tennessee Polytechnic Institute	Cookeville	046
Union University	Jackson	044
University of Chattanooga	Chattanooga	045
University of Tennessee	Knoxville	063
Texas		
Agricultural and Mechanical College of Texas	College Station	308
Austin College	Sherman	076
Southwest Texas State Teachers College	San Marcos	094
Texas Technological College	Lubbock	309
West Texas State Teachers College	Canyon	350
Utah		
Branch Agricultural College	Cedar City	318
Utah State Agricultural College	Logan	318
Virginia		
Lynchburg College	Lynchburg	014
Vermont		
Norwich University	Northfield	056
University of Vermont	Burlington	061
Washington		
Central Washington College of Education	Ellensburg	314
State College of Washington	Pullman	319
Wisconsin		
Beloit College	Beloit	095
Carroll College	Waukesha	075
Central State Teachers College	Stevens Point	097
Oshkosh State Teachers College	Oshkosh	096
State Teachers College	Eau Claire	301
State Teachers College	Milwaukee	351
Superior Teachers College	Superior	352
West Virginia		
Concord State Teachers College	Athens	015
Davis & Elkins College	Elkins	334
Marshall College	Huntington	047
West Virginia University	Morgantown	048
West Virginia Wesleyan College	Buckhannon	049

The histories of some school's detachments are available on microfilm at the Department of the Air Force, Air Force Historical Research Agency, Maxwell Air Force Base, Ala., as well as at the National Archives at College Park, Md.
*Participated in 1943 only.

TEN COMMANDMENTS

For Safe Flying

1. THOU SHALT NOT BECOME AIRBORNE WITHOUT CHECKING THY FUEL SUPPLY: It only takes a few minutes to gas up . . . it may save you a forced landing.

2. THOU SHALT NOT TAXI WITH CARELESSNESS: Taxi slowly and make S turns to clear the area in front of the nose. Know the proper use of the controls for taxiing in a strong wind.

3. THOU SHALT EVER TAKE HEED UNTO AIR TRAFFIC RULES: Keep a constant lookout for other aircraft. Follow the rules so that pilots of other planes will know what you are going to do.

4. THOU SHALT NOT MAKE FLAT TURNS: This is particularly important when making power-off turns. You steer with the ailerons, not the rudder.

5. THOU SHALT MAINTAIN THY SPEED LEST THE EARTH ARISE AND SMITE THEE: Don't be fooled by the increase in ground speed resulting from a downwind turn. Keep sufficient airspeed.

6. THOU SHALT NOT LET THY CONFIDENCE EXCEED THY ABILITY: Don't attempt instrument flying in adverse weather conditions unless you have the proper training and the necessary instruments. Instrument flying is a highly developed science. Don't pioneer.

7. THOU SHALT MAKE USE OF THY CARBURETOR HEATER: The carburetor heater is your friend. Know when to use it. Remember that it's easier to *prevent* ice in the carburetor than to eliminate it after it has formed.

8. THOU SHALT NOT PERFORM AEROBATICS AT LOW ALTITUDES: Aerobatics started near the ground may be completed six feet under the ground. There's safety in altitude.

9. THOU SHALT NOT ALLOW INDECISION IN THY JUDGMENT: Be certain! You can't afford to make errors of judgment. "I think I can make it" is on the list of famous last words.

10. THOU SHALT KNOW ALWAYS—THE GOOD PILOT IS THE SAFE PILOT: It's better to be an old pilot than a bold pilot.

Courtesy of
Piper Aircraft Corporation
Lock Haven, Penna.

Reprinted with permission from
Piper Aircraft Inc., Vero Beach, Fla.

Words of Flying Wisdom,
Collected by Fred "Posy" Thompson 1995

Flying is not simple. It is the hardest thing to learn and the easiest thing to do. Really, one never learns to fly, it is a continual process. You will hear a myriad of dos and don'ts from instructors. Some instructors are afraid to let you fly and some you are afraid to fly with. These words of wisdom are meant to keep us out of trouble.

If you can't afford to fly it right, be sure you can fly it wrong.

Don't trust nobody and don't do nothing dumb.

It's better to have a three-hour bladder and two hours of gas than vice versa.

It is easy to make a small fortune building airplanes as long as you start with a large fortune.

Flying is not dangerous but, like the sea, is unforgiving of ignorance and carelessness.

Never fly a plane that doesn't have the paint worn off the rudder petals.

Remember, you fly with your head not your hands.

If the engine quits, fly it to the ground, don't fall it to the ground.

If you force land, fly it as far as possible into the crash.

Never let an airplane take you someplace your brain didn't get to five minutes earlier.

Remember that a terminal forecast is a horoscope with numbers.

Keep looking around; there is always something you have missed.

It is better to be on the ground wishing you were flying than be flying wishing you were on the ground.

The purpose of the propeller is to keep the pilot cool. If you don't think so, stop the propeller and watch him sweat.

If something can go wrong it will; even if it can't, it will.

It doesn't do any good to stand on the brakes if you are already on your back.

A check ride should be like a skirt, short enough to be interesting, but long enough to cover everything.

A wheel landing is the trademark of the incompetent pilot.

Your new license is only a permit to learn to fly.

It's a good landing if you can still get the doors open.

No airplane is impressed by the ratings on your ticket.

The only time you can have too much fuel is when you are on FIRE.

Son, you're going to have to make up your mind about growing up to become a pilot. You can't do both.

There are old pilots and bold pilots, but there are no old bold pilots.

If the pilot survives the crash, you will never learn what really happened.

Flying is the hardest thing to learn and the easiest thing to do.

Forget all that stuff about left, thrust and drag; an airplane flies because of money.
If God had meant man to fly, he would have given him more money.

It used to be that flying was dangerous and sex was safe, now it is vice versa.

Flying Maneuvers
Taken from the Civil Aeronautics Administration Civil Pilot Training Manual
September 1941

This manual is designed primarily for the use of students taking the Elementary ground and flight courses and the Secondary flight course of the Civilian Pilot Training Program. The material contained herein therefore is outlined in accordance with the courses developed for that program. However, throughout the preparation of the manual, an effort has been made to make it equally valuable to all civilian student pilots as a standardized handbook of safe flying.

Part Two, Elementary Flight Course, covers the four stages (A, B, C and D) of the controlled Elementary flight course. Starting with the familiarization of the student with the airplane, this section follows, step by step, through the entire sequence of the various maneuvers comprising the complete course, ending with cross-country flying and the pilot's flight test.

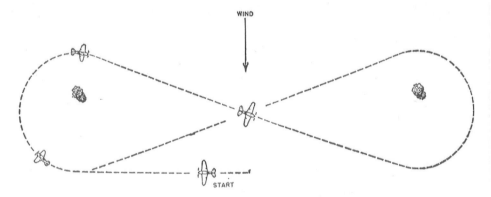

Figure 104. The pylon eight.

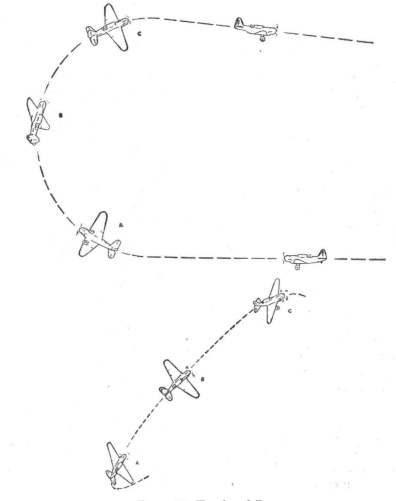

Figure 110. The chandelle.

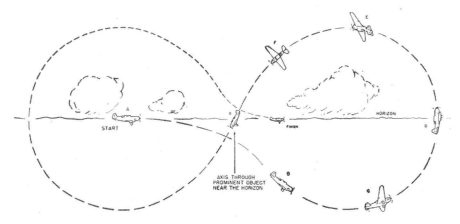

Figure 112. The lazy eight.

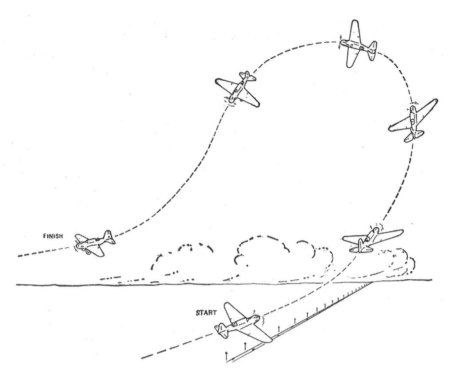

Figure 113. The wingover.

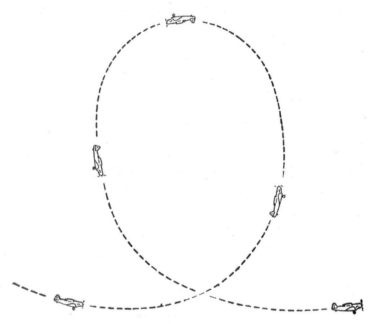

Figure 115. The loop.

Figure 116. The snap roll.

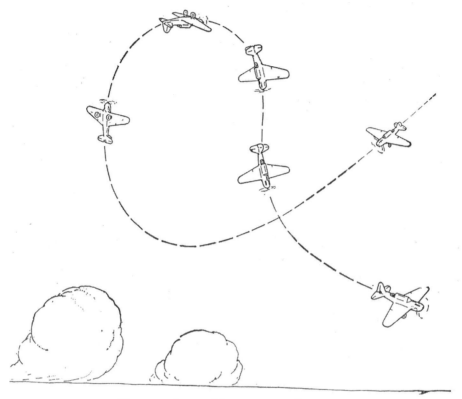

Figure 117. Loop with a quarter-roll recovery.

ACKNOWLEDGEMENTS

Until three years ago, I had no knowledge of the Civilian Pilot Training Program nor did I know that the Boards existed. All I had was one photo of my father in a military uniform and a child's memory of an airport. That doesn't make a book. Some of the contents of this project came from traditional sources for research. But most of this labor of love has come from dozens of generous and caring ordinary people, each contributing a small piece. Some had no obvious connection to the story and would not profit in any way, yet they graciously helped. I won't list them all—I'd likely miss too many. But several were there, night or day, when I called or e-mailed to ask for help: Fred "Posy" Thompson, Dick Double and Bill Raymer (answered aviation and airport questions and proofread); Joan Perrine Slack (was "my legs back home"); Anne and Bob Thompson; Joann Swartz (who has encouraged me since seventh-grade English); Matt Perkins (computer help); Curt Hazlett (cover design); Amy Clingensmith (editing, layout and graphics); Sue Solomon (indexing); Darren Shaw, Mark Burford and Matt Gable of Evangel Press; Mickey Russell of the Air Force Historical Research Agency, Piper Aircraft, Inc.; and the Hinckley Institute of Politics. To EAA Chapter #161 Grove City and the Rocky Filers, thank you for your hospitality. To those who wrote on behalf of the book: Dominick Pisano, Dick Jewell, Alexander Vraciu, Earl Tilford, Dick Mackell and Paul H. Poberezny, I am so grateful for your supportive words. Thank you to each and every one who graced this collaborative project, including the generous Patrons. You helped make *They Flew Proud*. Using the phrase Tom Brokaw helped popularize, it has been a true honor and privilege to have met and worked with so many of "The Greatest Generation" on this project.

● *Jane Gardner Birch*

PATRONS

Gold Patrons

Grove City College
Marshall Perkins
Anne and Bob Thompson
Sheri and Kirk Wheale

Silver Patrons

Kay McElroy Anderson
Connie and Lex Bailey
Dick Double
Sallie and Lynn Lyons

Bronze Patrons

Dick Bailey
Laurie and Dick Beech
Lynn Peck-Collins
Ray Cornelius
Penny Davis
Carol and Ray DeBonis
Una Hart
Bertha Mueller Heatley
Dorothy and Dick Mackell
Bob McGowan
Bill Mong
Morgan Perkins
Bill Raymer
Vicki and Jerry Schmid
Joyce Bowie Scott
Nancy and Harry Stein
Joann Swartz
Marilyn Terry
Eric Vanek
Eleanor Williamson

In Memorial

Gardner Birch by Hall, Meeks and Harbath
    namesakes
Gardner Birch by John Krofcheck
Grace Birch, wife of Gardner Birch, by Julie Birch
    Thompson
Robert and Edith Birch, Gardner's parents, by
    Julie Birch Thompson
Murl E. DeArment by Martha and Ella Mae
    Davis DeArment
Kathryn and Nelson Hassel by Virginia Birch
    Hall
George Frederick Hoaglin by Fred and Janet
    Wolbert Hoaglin
Brenton Holter by daughters Brenda, Karen and
    Shari
Jack E. Mars by daughter Allyn Mars Rishel
Emerson and Jack Perrine by Joan Perrine Slack
Gene Rodgers by Jeanne and Ron Rodgers
Robert "Scotty" Scott by Fred "Posy" Thompson
Doris and Russell Smith by Russell Smith
John M. Subject by John R. Subject

PHOTO CREDITS

Many contributed photos or visuals for this book, too many to mention individually, lest I forget someone. Special tribute goes to Martha DeArment for donating Fuzzy's personal photo album with its many pictures from the airport during the Civilian Pilot Training Program. Special thanks to commercial photographer Richard Smaltz, New York City, for his photos of the Boards. He had to literally remove them from the walls to get quality images. Richard, a graduate of Rochester Institute of Technology, studied under Ansel Adams. And thanks to Bill Collins, Annapolis, Md., for his many attempts to get an image of me that would be worthy of the book. Also thank you to the Piper Corporation and to the Hinckley Institute of Politics for giving us a glimpse into the history of the CPTP.

INDEX